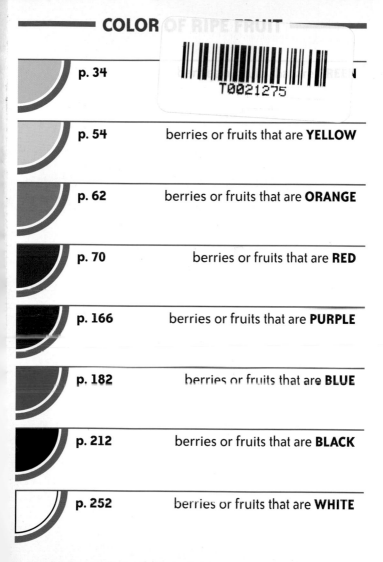

COLOR OF RIPE FRUIT

Wild BERRIES & FRUITS

MINNESOTA, WISCONSIN & MICHIGAN

Field Guide

2nd Edition

by Teresa Marrone

Adventure Publications
Cambridge, Minnesota

ACKNOWLEDGMENTS

Thanks to Gustave Axelson for his review of the book.

Cover and book design by Jonathan Norberg

Flower anatomy illustration by Julie Martinez

Edited by Brett Ortler

Photo credits by photographer and page number:
Cover photos: blueberry, buttonbush, black raspberry and rose hips by Teresa Marrone

All photos by Teresa Marrone, unless noted.
Alfred Cook: 63 **Will Cook:** 171 (bottom right)
Shannon Hammonds: 193 **Mary Hopson:** 135
Emmet Judziewicz/UW Stevens Point Herbarium: 195 (both)
Mike Krebill: 221 **Louis-M. Landry:** 97 (fruit)
Robbin Moran: 123 **Walter Muma:** 237, 265 (both)
Don Poggensee: 71 **Rob Routledge, Sault College,
Bugwood.org:** 231 (inset) **Stan Tekiela:** 97 (main)
Ryann Waite: 59 (inset) **www.sunfarm.com:** 79
www.tafoni.net: 107 (top) **www.tripplebrookfarm.com:** 103 (both)

10 9 8 7 6

Wild Berries & Fruits Field Guide: Minnesota, Wisconsin and Michigan

First Edition 2009
Second Edition 2018
Copyright © 2009 and 2018 by Teresa Marrone
Published by Adventure Publications
An imprint of AdventureKEEN
310 Garfield Street South
Cambridge, Minnesota 55008
(800) 678-7006
www.adventurepublications.net
Printed in China
ISBN 978-1-59193-796-8 (pbk.); ISBN 978-1-59193-797-5 (ebook)

TABLE OF CONTENTS

ABOUT THIS BOOK

Numerous field guides are available to aid in flower identification, but few address the fruiting stage of the plant. Those that do usually add a footnote or a small photo of the fruit. But the fruiting stage is critical to the plant and interesting to observers of nature as well. This book is specifically about that glorious stage in a plant's life when it fulfills its purpose by producing fruits to help it reproduce.

This book was written with the forager in mind, and especially for foragers interested in taking home their finds and using them in recipes and in the kitchen. Always be certain of your identification when gathering wild fruits (or any other wild edible); if possible, check with a knowledgeable forager who is familiar with the plants in your area.

In addition to showing edible berries and fruits, this book also identifies those berries and fruits which are inedible—even toxic. This information is critical to anyone who is faced with an unknown plant and wishes to know if its fruit is edible. It's also just plain interesting to see all the fascinating and, often, lovely fruits produced by plants, whether that fruit is edible or not.

Photos in this book focus primarily on the fruits, in all their up-close-and-personal glory. However, plant structure and leaf form are also critical to proper identification. The photos here attempt to show the key identification points of each plant; this information is also covered in the text that accompanies each photo. Features that are key to distinguishing a plant from one with similar appearance are in green type in the text; study these points with particular care when looking at a plant.

Habitat and season are also important when attempting to identify a plant. Both of these are covered in the text. Range maps for each species show approximate locations in Minnesota, Wisconsin and Michigan where each plant is likely to be found. Helpful information that allows the reader to compare similar plants provides additional insight that will aid in positive identification. Finally, each plant account includes short notes, which may feature interesting tidbits about the plant, how it has been used for food or medicine, or information on how the plant is used by birds and other wildlife.

Common names of plants are often confusing. People in different areas use different names for the same plant, and, sometimes, the same common name is used for two—or more—very different plants. All plant accounts in this book include the common name usually used by the United States Department of Agriculture, and occasionally another common name. More importantly, the scientific name is listed for each species; this is the most definitive nomenclature of all.

THE RANGE MAPS

The maps showing plant ranges are based on information from the United States Department of Agriculture, the United States Geological Survey, the United States Forest Service, and Early Detection & Distribution Mapping System (see pg. 266 for website addresses). These sources have been supplemented with state-specific surveys from natural-resources agencies, universities and herbariums, as well as the author's personal knowledge and experience.

Range maps are a useful tool, but are not an absolute authority. Plants rarely follow state or county lines, but most plant surveyors do when reporting their data to the USDA or other authorities. Further, some counties have not submitted data or been surveyed, and so do not appear on the lists used by government agencies. The maps in this book are approximations, and it is possible to find a plant in an area not shown on the range map (or, conversely, to be unable to find a plant in an area indicated on the map). In some cases, county-specific data is not available, yet the plant is known to grow in the state. In such cases, the state is colored with a lighter shade of the color used in that section; this indicates that the plant is present in the state, but does not show specific areas where it may be found.

WHAT IS A FRUIT?

Since this book is all about fruit, it's worth discussing exactly what that term means in the context of the book. At its most basic, a fruit is the ripened part of a plant that disperses seeds; this includes things like pea pods, wheat heads and nuts. In everyday usage, however, most of us consider only fleshy, juicy, seed-bearing structures, such as blueberries, watermelon and apples, to be "fruit." The short and fairly non-scientific discussion that follows will provide helpful reference for the discussion of various fruit types discussed later.

Like most living things, plants have male and female parts. Depending on species, they may exist together in one flower as illustrated below, or may grow in distinct male or female flowers. (Sometimes the male and female parts don't look anything like this, as with pine trees; then again, these plants don't produce what we think of as fruit.) The female part of the plant, at the center of the flower, is collectively called the *pistil*. It consists of an ovary, topped with a long style, capped with the stigma. The ovary is a case containing one or more carpels, which are ovule-bearing structures, and contain one or more ovules, or eggs; typically, several carpels are fused together within the ovary, but in a few cases the carpel is single.

The male part of the plant is collectively called the *stamen*. It consists of the pollen-bearing element called the anther, which is supported by the filament, a thin structure that raises the anther above the base of the flower. (The flower petals are there to attract pollinators, by the way—the plant world's version of the little black dress.)

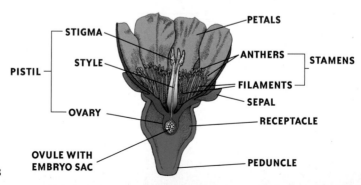

Seeds develop when pollen is introduced to ripe eggs. This service is performed by insects, animals or the wind; regardless of the method, the pollen is deposited onto the sticky stigma, where it germinates, sending the male nuclei down the style to fertilize the eggs. The ovary swells as the seeds mature. The result of all this activity is the fruit—a fleshy structure carrying the fertilized seeds.

Within that narrow definition, there are several types of fruit. Here are short, simple definitions of the types of fruits that are included in this book; please also look at pg. 19 to see what is *not* included.

BERRIES

A berry is a simple fleshy fruit containing one or more carpels (ovule-bearing structures), each with one or more seeds. The seed coating, or endocarp, is relatively soft. Examples include grapes (pg. 170), gooseberries (pgs. 46, 174, 226), currants (pgs. 120, 228) and blueberries (pgs. 190, 202).

Grapes

Gooseberries

Currants

Blueberries

DRUPES

A drupe, sometimes called a stone fruit, is a simple fleshy fruit with a seed (or on occasion, seeds) contained in a hard pit, or stone. The hard outside of the pit is the endocarp (seed coating). Examples include plums (pg. 154), autumn olives (pg. 146) and chokecherries (pg. 136).

American wild plum

Autumn olive

Common chokecherry

COMPOUND DRUPES

A compound drupe is a fleshy fruit formed from a single flower, but composed of many drupes, each containing one seed. Compound drupes are typically thought of as "seedy" because they contain so many seeds, each with its own endocarp (seed coating). Examples include red raspberries (pg. 116) and blackberries (pg. 234).

Red raspberry

Blackberry

Mulberry

MULTIPLE FRUIT

An unusual fruit structure in which a single fruit is formed from multiple flowers that grow closely together in a cluster. The only multiple fruit in this book is the mulberry (pg. 152). Figs and pineapples are multiple fruits that don't grow in our region.

POMES

A pome is a pseudocarp, a simple fruit with flesh developed from the receptacle (the end of the flower stalk) rather than the ovary. In pomes, the receptacle surrounds the ovary, and seeds are contained in the carpel, which becomes papery. Examples in this book include crabapples (pg. 162), hawthorns (pg. 160), mountain ash (pg. 68) and serviceberries (pg. 178).

Crabapple

Hawthorn

Mountain ash

Serviceberry

OTHER TYPES OF FRUIT

Strawberry

Pseudocarps are fruits whose flesh develops from a part other than the ovary. Pomes (pg. 11) are one type. Another is the strawberry (pg. 72); unlike a pome, however, the strawberry carries its seeds on the surface rather than in the center of the fruit.

Wild cucumber

Pepos are berry-like fruits with a very tough rind developed from the receptacle (in most fruits, the skin is developed from the ovary). Wild cucumber (pg. 44) is a pepo that is in this book; others which are not in this book are melons and gourds.

Purple trillium

Capsules are dry, non-fleshy fruits that split at maturity to scatter their seeds. Most capsule fruits don't resemble anything we'd think of as fruit and are not included here; however, several, including trillium (pg. 76) have a large, fleshy capsule that looks like fruit, so they are included.

Common juniper

Cones are fruits that consist of scales (sporophylls) arranged in an overlapping or spiral fashion around a central core; seeds are developed between the scales. Common juniper (pg. 196) and eastern red cedar (pg. 206) are included in this book because their cones look berry-like.

HOW FRUITS ARE ARRANGED ON THE STEM

Fruits may grow singly on a stem, or in clusters. Locations also vary; fruits may grow at the ends of branches, along the branches, or in leaf axils. Here are a few of the common arrangements and locations.

A *raceme* is a cluster of fruit growing on a central stem; each fruit has its own stalk, and all stalks are of equal length. At left is a raceme of black cherries. Racemes can also be branched, with each branch having a small raceme; this is called a *panicle*.

A rounded *umbrella-like cluster*, called an *umbel*, contains numerous fruit stalks that grow from a common point on the main fruiting stem. All stalks are the same length, so the cluster is rounded.

Black cherry

The highbush cranberry shown at right is an example. Another type of umbrella-like cluster is called a *corymb*; in this arrangement, fruit stalks vary in length so that all fruits are aligned in a flat-topped cluster.

Highbush cranberry

The *leaf axil* is the point at which the leaf joins the stem; many fruits are attached at the axils. At right are glossy buckthorn fruits growing from the leaf axils.

Glossy buckthorn

Fruits also grow at the end of the stem; at left is a cluster of silky dogwood fruits growing at the end of a stem.

Silky dogwood

LEAF FORM AND ARRANGEMENT

Leaves are one of the most important features to consider when attempting to identify a plant. Their shape, the way they attach to the plant, characteristics of the edge, and, of course, size and color must all be considered. Botanists use many terms to describe these things in exacting detail; this book does not reach so far, using terms geared to the layperson. Here is a brief overview of some of these terms.

Amur honeysuckle

Form and arrangement are the first characteristics to look at. The leaves of this honeysuckle are *simple*—a single leaf blade is attached to the stem of the plant. The leaf is narrowly oval, with a rounded base and pointed tip. Looking closer, we see that the leaf has a short *petiole*—the stemlet that attaches the leaf to the stem. The leaf is attached *oppositely*—directly across the stem from another leaf. Its edge is *smooth*, not jagged or toothy. It is deep green and glossy above. The *midrib*—the long line that divides the leaf in two—is pale.

Gooseberry

Although the gooseberry leaves at left are also called simple, there's a lot more going on. They are *lobed*, meaning that each leaf, although whole and undivided, has several distinct sections, rather like a maple leaf. The petiole (stemlet) is much longer than that of the honeysuckle above. The leaves are arranged *alternately* on the stem, with some distance between the points where each leaf attaches to the stem. Leaf veins are noticeable but not prominent, and the midvein does not stand out as on the honeysuckle leaf. Leaf color is medium green above, and the surface is somewhat *rough*; leaf edges have *rounded teeth*, and the base is broad.

Black raspberry

Compound leaves look like a small stem with numerous leaves; the entire grouping is called a *blade*. Individual leaves on each blade are called *leaflets*. The blade is a true leaf, with a bud at its base; leaflets don't have buds. This black raspberry has three-part compound leaves—each blade has three leaflets, which have *sharply toothed edges*. Compound leaves can have a dozen or more leaflets on each blade. If they are arranged in a row along the blade stem, the blade is said to be pinnately compound; see mountain ash on pg. 68 for an example.

Some compound leaves are even more complicated, consisting of several compound leaves attached to the blade stem. The white baneberry pictured at right has *doubly-compound* leaves: The blade has three compound leaves, each with five to seven leaflets. This plant has three doubly-compound leaves: The one at the top, which also is bearing the fruiting stalk, and the two that are going off to the sides near the bottom of the photo.

White baneberry

Virginia creeper

The final type of compound leaf is called *palmately compound*. As shown by the leaves of this Virginia creeper, the leaflets all radiate from a central point, rather than growing on a blade stem.

Note that characteristics of the individual leaves shown here, other than leaf form, are not always as shown. For example, a simple leaf can have a long or short petiole (or no petiole); its edges may be pointed or smooth, and it may grow alternately.

15

LEAF ATTACHMENT

The previous pages showed some examples of leaf attachment; this page gives additional examples of those, as well as a few others that were not shown. Note that the text discusses the attachment of a leaf to the stem, but the same attachment styles could also apply to the attachment of a leaflet to a blade stem (on a compound leaf).

Crabapple

Many leaves are attached to the stem by a *petiole*, which can be defined as a leaf stemlet. Petioles can be long or short, smooth or hairy, round or flattened, and any color found in nature. The petioles on the crabapple leaves shown at left are long, smooth and greenish.

Some leaves are *sessile*—they attach directly to the stem. The rose twisted stalk shown below left is an example of this. *Perfoliate* leaves, like those of the large-flowered bellwort shown below right, have a base that extends slightly beyond the stem, giving the impression that the stem is growing up through the leaf.

Rose twisted stalk

Large flowered bellwort

Clasping leaves have no petiole (stemlet); the base of the leaf clasps, or slightly surrounds the stem, but does not extend beyond it. Smooth Solomon's seal, pictured at right, is an example of a clasping leaf.

Smooth Solomon's seal

Purple trillium

Sometimes, three or more leaves grow from a common point of attachment. This style of leaf arrangement is called *whorled*, and is seen in the trillium photo at left.

To the botanist, leaf attachment and leaf arrangement are different discussions; for the layperson, the distinction is not important. The whorled example seems to cross into both categories.

LEAF SHAPES

Leaves and leaflets take numerous shapes; here are the most common. Note that leaves may taper on one or both ends, may have rounded or heart-shaped bases with pointed tips, or any number of combinations.

Lowbush blueberry

Oval leaves (sometimes called elliptic leaves) are the most familiar. At left are the oval leaves of blueberries.

Lance-shaped or sword-like leaves are long and slender; often, sides are almost parallel for much of the leaves' length. Below left are the lance-shaped leaves of false Solomon's seal.

Paddle-shaped leaves are narrow at the base, widening at or above the midpoint; they typically have a rounded tip. Below right are the paddle-shaped leaves of clintonia.

False Solomon's seal

Clintonia

SAFETY AND PLANT IDENTIFICATION

If you are using this book to identify plants just for pleasure, that's great; hopefully, you will find what you're looking for and may even enjoy keeping a life list of fruits spotted. However, if you are planning to eat any of the fruits you identify, it is critical to follow good identification practices. Before sampling a plant's fruit, determine the plant's overall structure, its color, its leaf and stem arrangement, fruit appearance and characteristics. The photos and text in this book are as clear and concise as possible; however, they are not exhaustive. Sometimes, a plant looks slightly different than those photographed, and identification becomes a bit of a guessing game. It's prudent to consult more than one guidebook before consuming something you've foraged, and I strongly urge you to do so. The Helpful Resources on pgs. 266–267 will give you some sources that may be helpful. This extra effort is worth it; a mistake could cause illness or, in rare cases, death.

It's also important to note that individual reaction to foods varies; to some, the everyday peanut is a ballpark snack, while to others, it can cause life-threatening complications if ingested. Reactions to wild foods are not always well documented or predictable; when you're eating an unfamiliar wild food, try just a small portion at first.

Also, remember that many wild foods are edible only at a certain stage of growth, or with certain special preparations. That information is beyond the scope of this book; however, the notes and information with each species account point out possible issues with the various fruits you may find. If the text has any indications that special preparations may be required, or that ripeness is critical to edibility, it is your responsibility to learn what is required to make certain your foraged fruits are edible and safe.

Some fruits are edible but not palatable; these are noted as "edible" in most cases, although in a few cases they are noted as "not edible" because they really aren't worth experimenting with. Others may cause

stomach upset or other relatively minor difficulties; these are noted as "not edible." Some, however, can kill if enough is ingested; and in a few cases, the amount is shockingly little. These plants are listed as "toxic" and contain the skull-and-crossbones symbol at left. Pay attention to this. It's not worth taking chances.

WHAT IS NOT INCLUDED IN THIS BOOK

In general, the fruits included in this book are those which most people would identify as fruits. Capsules, such as those produced by poppies, maple-tree wings (samaras), and dry seeds such as sunflower seeds and wheat kernels, would not likely be considered as fruits, so they are not in this book. Here are some other things that are not included.

Nuts, such as these shagbark hickories, are large, dry fruits with hard seedcoats; they usually contain a single seed. Nuts are indehiscent, meaning that they remain closed when mature.

Legumes are pods, often quite narrow, that contain pea-like or bean-like seeds. Legumes are dehiscent, meaning that they dry out and split open, releasing their seeds. Pods of American vetch are pictured at left.

Follicles are dry, dehiscent fruits that dry out and split on one side to scatter their seeds. The fruit of a milkweed, a very common follicle, is pictured at left.

Galls are not a fruit, but rather a swelling in the stem of a plant caused by an insect. The round bulge on this anemone could be easily mistaken for a fruit.

NOT RIPE YET!

Most berries and fruits start out green, changing to another color when they are ripe; a few, however, remain green even when ripe. Others are a color other than green even though they are still unripe. This book is organized by the color of the ripe fruit. If you encounter a plant that has green (or obviously unripe) fruit on it, how can you find it in this book if you don't know what color it will be when it *is* ripe? This is of particular interest if the fruit will be edible when it's ripe; you can note the location of the unripe fruit and return later in the season to harvest it.

To help, here are photos of some edible berries and fruits in the unripe stage, along with information that points you to the correct page in this book. Note that gooseberries (pgs. 46, 174, 226) are edible in both the green and the ripe stages, so they appear in more than one color section.

Lowbush blueberry (pg. 190)

Wild grape (pg. 170)

Red raspberry (pg. 116)

Blackberry (pg. 234)

Common elderberry (pg. 176)

Thimbleberry (pg. 118)

Rose hip (pg. 124)

Highbush cranberry (pg. 142)

Sand cherry (pg. 224)

American wild plum (pg. 154)

BE CERTAIN, BE SAFE: WILD GRAPES

Wild grapes are a prime wild edible; they're delicious and abundant. However, several other vining plants in our area have inedible or toxic fruits that appear somewhat similar to wild grapes. Fortunately, it's easy to distinguish between them if you pay attention when harvesting.

Below is a photo of riverbank grapes (pg. 170). On the next page, you'll find photos of some fruits that appear similar. Key identification points also help you distinguish between grapes and these other fruits.

Riverbank grape

Canada moonseed (pg. 172)

Five-leaved ivy (pg. 188)

Smilax (pg. 218)

LEAVES

Grape: Three to five deep to shallow lobes, toothed edges

Canada moonseed: Three to seven shallow lobes, smooth edges

Five-leaved ivy: Palmately compound (typically 5-part), coarsely toothed edges

Smilax: Heart-shaped or oval, smooth edges

TENDRILS

Grape: Coiling tendrils

Canada moonseed: No tendrils

Five-leaved ivy: Tendrils with two or more branches

Smilax: Varies with species

FRUITS

Grape: Purplish with a bloom; large, tight cluster of numerous berries on sturdy, greenish fruit stalk; two to six seeds per berry (delicious)

Canada moonseed: Purplish with a bloom; long, thin fruit stalk with loose clusters of fruits; single flat, crescent-shaped seed (toxic)

Five-leaved ivy: Bluish-purple with a bloom; loose clusters of berries on hot-pink stemlets (toxic)

Smilax: Bluish-black with a bloom; rounded cluster on long, stiff stalk (edible)

RIPENING CALENDAR FOR EDIBLE FRUIT

	May	June
Gooseberries (pgs. 46, 174, 226)		
Ground-plum milkvetch (pg. 70)		
Strawberry (pg. 72)		
Serviceberry (pg. 178)		
Red mulberry (pg. 152)		
Black raspberry (pg. 222)		
White mulberry (pg. 152)		
Blueberries (pgs. 190, 202)		
Fragrant sumac (pg. 114)		
Crabapple, apple (pg. 162)		
Russet buffaloberry (pg. 134)		
Dewberries (pgs. 84, 232)		
Mock strawberry (pg. 90)		
Hawthorn (pg. 160)		
Black huckleberry (pg. 230)		
Red raspberry (pg. 116)		
Currants (pgs. 120, 228)		
Mountain fly honeysuckle (pg. 194)		
Sand cherry (pg. 224)		
Thimbleberry (pg. 118)		
Bunchberry (pg. 86)		
Black cherry (pg. 248)		
Dwarf bilberry (pg. 192)		
Pin cherry (pg. 156)		
Chokecherry (pg. 136)		
Sumac (pgs. 164, 180)		
Mayapple (pg. 54)		

Timing may vary by several weeks from the southern to the northern part of our area, and also may vary from year to year depending on weather. Date ranges shown here are

24

FLOWER / UNRIPE / RIPE / PERSISTS THROUGH WINTER

July	August	September	October	Winter

* *edible when green in color*

an average; fruits in any given area may ripen a week or two earlier—or later—than shown.

25

RIPENING CALENDAR FOR EDIBLE FRUIT

	May	June
Bearberry *(pg. 108)*		
Blackberry *(pg. 234)*		
Ground cherry *(pg. 56)*		
Highbush cranberry *(pg. 142)*		
Blackhaw *(pg. 246)*		
Starry false Solomon's seal *(pg. 38)*		
Common pear *(pg. 48)*		
Bastard toadflax *(pg. 82)*		
Common elderberry *(pg. 176)*		
American wild plum *(pg. 154)*		
Creeping snowberry *(pg. 258)*		
Mountain ash *(pg. 68)*		
Partridge berry *(pg. 98)*		
Russian olive *(pg. 60)*		
Northern spicebush *(pg. 148)*		
Pawpaw *(pg. 50)*		
Withe-rod *(pg. 204)*		
Chokeberry *(pg. 240)*		
Cranberry *(pg. 106)*		
Rose hip *(pg. 124)*		
Autumn olive *(pg. 146)*		
Wild grape *(pg. 170)*		
Hackberry *(pg. 250)*		
Nannyberry *(pg. 246)*		
Blackgum *(pg. 210)*		
Creeping wintergreen *(pg. 110)*		

Timing may vary by several weeks from the southern to the northern part of our area, and also may vary from year to year depending on weather. Date ranges shown here are an average; fruits in any given area may ripen a week or two earlier—or later—than shown.

July	August	September	October	Winter

HOW TO USE THIS BOOK

1. When you find a plant with fruits, pay attention to **fruit color** first. Use the colored quarter-circles at the top corner of the left-hand pages to find the corresponding section.

SMALL
WOODY SHRUB

2. Next, identify the **form of the plant**: is it a tender leafy plant, a shrub (small or large?), a vine or a tree? Flip through the color section until you find the proper form, using the icon at the top of the page.

3. Look through the **photos** in this section and see if you find similar fruits. If you can't, look in the color sections before and after the section you're in; if you are looking at a red fruit, but don't see anything like it, go to the orange section or to the purple section. Color judgment is subjective, and individual specimens may vary slightly, so you may have to look for the fruit in several color sections.

Mountain ash

It's also possible that you've found unripe fruit, and since this book shows fruits in the ripe stage, you might not be looking in the right color section. Most fruits are green when immature, ripening to a different

Black raspberry

color; but some pass through several colors before fully ripening. Black raspberries (pg. 222), for example, start out green and ripen to black; in between they turn yellow, salmon-orange, bright red, and purplish-red. Other fruits undergo similar transformations. Once you find something that looks similar—even if it's the wrong color—proceed to the next step.

4. Look at the **range map** icon at the top of the page to determine whether the plant is found in your area. Use these range maps as an approximation, as there are few official sources of information pertaining to wild plants, and no resource is all-inclusive.

ALTERNATE
LEAVES

5. When you find a photograph that appears similar to the fruit you've found (even if the color is not quite right), and the plant is the correct form, take a look at the **leaves** to see if they grow opposite one another on the stem, alternately on the stem, or in a whorl. This distinction is often the main key to properly identifying a plant.

6. Now read the full description, paying particular attention to any text that is in green; this color is used to point out key features that distinguish a plant from those with similar appearances. Also **study the "Compare"** section; here, you'll find information about plants that have similarities to the one pictured, along with page references for those which appear in this book. By following these references, you may sometimes find a photo showing the fruit you've found in a more ripened state; the description on that page will help you to identify the plant, even if you're looking at it in its unripe state.

SUMMER

7. To help determine when a fruit ripens, we've included a **season** icon at the top of the page. This will tell you the approximate season you're likely to find ripe berries or fruits and can help narrow down the possibilities when there are a number of look-alike fruits and berries.

8. Finally, the **thumb tab** at the top indicates whether a plant is toxic, not edible, edible, or delicious.

A species indicated as **toxic** has fruits that are highly poisonous and should not be eaten under any circumstances. The corresponding photo bears a skull and crossbones symbol for good reason; do not sample any part of a plant bearing this symbol. Species indicated as **not edible** bear fruit which, while not highly toxic, may cause sickness upon ingestion or have other negative side effects. Species indicated as **edible** bear fruits that are just that: edible. Some are bland but handy to know about as survival food, while others have a minor place in the forager's kitchen. Species indicated as **delicious** are the berries and fruits many people seek out. Blueberries, raspberries, and chokecherries are just a few of the many delicious wild fruits found in Minnesota, Wisconsin, and Michigan. Unlike the fruits simply marked as edible, these are the best wild edibles the region has to offer.

Here's an example; follow along to see if you can identify this fruit.

The plant has fruit that is primarily red, and it is a large shrub (you can't see that in the photo above, but in the field, the form is obvious). Go to the red section of the book (starting on pg. 70), and flip to the beginning of the section that lists large shrubs (pg. 130).

LARGE
WOODY SHRUB

Eleven large shrub species are listed in the red section. Three of them (red elderberry, prickly ash and winged euonymus) can be eliminated right away, because the fruit doesn't look at all like this.

ALTERNATE
LEAVES

You notice that the leaves on this plant are alternate, spaced along the stem rather than across from one another. This eliminates russet buffaloberries and bush honeysuckles. Highbush cranberries also have opposite leaves, which also happen to look like maple leaves, so that's eliminated for sure. Five species remain as possibilities.

Examining the leaves more closely, you note that they have fine teeth. This eliminates glossy buckthorn, autumn olive and northern spicebush, whose leaves have smooth edges. You also note that the fruits of your plant grow in hanging clusters with multiple fruits, but the three plants you're eliminating here all have single fruits or small, tight bunches of fruits growing in leaf axils. Fruits of autumn olive are speckled with silver, and northern spicebush has a distinct, spicy fragrance; your plant has neither of these characteristics.

Two choices remain: common chokecherry and winterberry. First, double-check the range maps for both species. Chokecherry (pg. 136) is found all over the tri-state region. Winterberry (pg. 144) has a more restricted range, which may eliminate it as a possibility depending on where you are. The description for winterberry mentions that the leaves are sharply toothed on the edges, but your plant has fine teeth; in addition, the fruit clusters on winterberry are small clusters growing in leaf axils rather than a hanging cluster. Studying the text on the chokecherry page, it seems likely that you've found a chokecherry.

To confirm your identification, study the "Compare" text on pg. 136 to see what other plants resemble this one. Looking at the photos of black cherry (pg. 248) and pin cherry (pg. 156), you see that although the fruit is similar, those plants have leaves that are much narrower. In addition, your plant doesn't have any hairs on the midrib underneath, so it's not a black cherry; and the fruit on your plant is growing in a hanging cluster (a raceme) so it's not a pin cherry. The leaves do look like those of the serviceberry (pg. 178), but the fruit on your plant does not have a crown on the bottom.

Congratulations! You've found a common chokecherry, a prime wild edible fruit that is usually juiced to make a delicious jelly.

SMALL
WOODY SHRUB

ALTERNATE
COMPOUND
LEAVES

SUMMER

Common Name

Scientific name

HABITAT: General environment in which the plant is typically found in our area, including light and moisture requirements

GROWTH: The growth form of the plant in our area, ranging from small, tender plants, to vines, to small or large shrubs, to trees

LEAVES: Description of the plant's leaves, including leaf style and shape, arrangement on the plant, attachment to the main stem, and color of the leaves

FRUIT: Description of the fruit, including type (berry, pome, drupe or other), color, arrangement, appearance and edibility information

SEASON: When the plant bears ripe fruit in our area

COMPARE: Plants or fruits with similar attributes, including characteristics that differentiate them

NOTES: Interesting facts about the plant, including harvesting tips for edible plants, notes on other parts of the plant that may be edible, historical or modern-day medicinal uses, and miscellaneous tips and facts

SAMPLE

TENDER
LEAFY PLANT

ALTERNATE
LEAVES

SPRING

Large-Flowered Bellwort

Uvularia grandiflora

HABITAT: Thrives in shady, deciduous forests with ample moisture.

GROWTH: This native plant sends up round stems from underground rhizomes (root-bearing stems). Mature plants divide into 2 or 3 stems; each of these stems will bear a flower. Early in the season, the plant is upright, 1 to 1½ feet tall, with droopy leaves and yellow 6-petaled flowers that appear dehydrated. When the flowers drop off, the stem becomes longer and stiffer, and starts to recline; at this stage, the stem's zigzag character becomes more noticeable.

LEAVES: Perfoliate, lance-shaped leaves grow alternately on the zigzag stem. Leaves are 3 to 6 inches long, smooth on top, with 3 to 5 parallel veins; undersides are covered with downy white hairs.

FRUIT: Each mature stem has one flowering stalk that grows from a leaf axil near the end of the stem. A perfoliate leaf grows about midway up the flowering stalk; the fruit, a lobed, 3-part triangular green capsule about ½ inch long, replaces the flower at the end of the stalk and rests atop the leaf. The fruit is inedible, but the young shoots of the plant can be cooked like asparagus (but only when identification is certain, as other shoots which resemble bellwort are toxic).

SEASON: Bellwort flowers in spring, and the fruit follows in late spring.

COMPARE: A related native species, sessile bellwort or wild oats (*U. sessilifolia*), looks similar, but the fruit has a pointed tip, and the leaves are not perfoliate; instead, they are attached to the stem by a small petiole (stemlet). Rose twisted stalk and the various Solomon's seals resemble large-flowered bellwort, but can be distinguished from it without much difficulty. Please see the text with common false Solomon's seal (unripe) on pg. 36 for further information.

NOTES: Large-flowered bellwort flowers are a rich pollen source for a variety of bees. The plant is a favored browse of deer; where there is an over-abundance of deer, colonies of large-flowered bellwort may be damaged or destroyed.

green = key identification feature

TENDER
LEAFY PLANT

ALTERNATE
LEAVES

SUMMER

Common False
Solomon's Seal (unripe)   *Maianthemum racemosum*

HABITAT: This native plant is common and widespread in deciduous or mixed-wood forests throughout our area. It also grows in waste ground.

GROWTH: The single stem usually grows in a zigzag fashion, bending slightly at each leaf axil; it may be up to 3 feet in length. When young, the stem is upright, but as the plant matures, it typically reclines until it is almost horizontal.

LEAVES: Bright green, shiny leaves are lance-shaped, with a sharp tip at the end; they are up to 8 inches long and about one-third as wide. Leaves are attached directly to the stem in an alternate arrangement, and feature deep parallel veins curving from base to tip.

FRUIT: Numerous smooth, round berries grow in a long cluster at the end of the stem; each berry is about ⅛ inch across. When unripe, berries are greenish with tiny purple blotches. Ripe berries are deep red and somewhat translucent. The berries are inedible.

SEASON: Unripe berries are present most of the summer; berries ripen in late summer.

COMPARE: A number of plants have similar leaves and growth habit, but a closer look distinguishes them. Rose twisted stalk (pg. 80) and smooth Solomon's seal (pg. 184) bear fruits at the leaf axils rather than at the end of the stem; smooth Solomon's seal's stems do not zigzag. Starry false Solomon's seal (pg. 38) has a cluster of fruits at the end of the stem, but the plant is shorter, generally 2 feet or less, and the leaves are narrower; it tends to be more upright rather than reclining, and the fruits are fewer and pumpkin-shaped. Large-flowered bellwort (pg. 34) is also short, up to 2 feet tall; leaves are perfoliate, and each stem bears a single triangular-shaped fruit.

NOTES: Another common name for this plant is feathery false lily of the valley. Some scientific texts list it as *Smilacina racemosa*.

green = key identification feature

Ripe berries

TENDER
LEAFY PLANT

ALTERNATE
LEAVES

SUMMER

Starry False
Solomon's Seal (unripe)

Maianthemum stellatum

HABITAT: Cool, moist forests; often adjacent to streams, also found in sandy areas near marshes. Starry false Solomon's seal is often one of the first plants to grow after a forest fire. It is a native plant.

GROWTH: A single stem grows from an underground rhizome (root-bearing stem) to a height of 1 to 2 feet. The plant arches somewhat, but is not droopy.

LEAVES: Lance-shaped leaves, up to 6 inches long and one-quarter as wide, grow alternately from the main stem, which appears to **bend slightly** at each leaf axil. Leaves attach directly to the stem, and are stiff and bluish-green, with prominent parallel veins; they are smooth on top and may be slightly hairy underneath.

FRUIT: A short raceme (a cluster of multiple fruits) of berries grows at the end of the plant. Unripe berries are **green with dark red stripes**, and are shaped rather like a **small, squat pumpkin** about 5/16 inch across. The berries ripen to dark red; they may retain subtle striping. The ripe berries are edible raw or cooked, but have a laxative effect if eaten when raw. They have a bittersweet flavor, and are reportedly high in vitamin C.

SEASON: Star-shaped white flowers, which give the plant its common name, appear from mid-spring to early summer. The green berries follow, and are present on the plant through late summer.

COMPARE: Please see the discussion of similar plants listed on pg. 36. Starry false Solomon's seal is most likely to be confused with common false Solomon's seal, which is generally a **larger** plant, with more leaves and a larger number of berries in the **terminal cluster**; also, its berries are **tiny and round**, and are greenish speckled with purple when unripe.

NOTES: Starry false Solomon's seal is sometimes listed in references as *Smilacina stellata*. Ruffed grouse eat the ripe berries in autumn.

green = key identification feature

Ripe fruit

TENDER
LEAFY PLANT

ALTERNATE
LEAVES

SUMMER
TO FALL

*see below

Jimsonweed

Datura stramonium, D. wrightii

HABITAT: Two species of this toxic plant appear in our region: *Datura stramonium*, the common variety which is also called thorn apple; and *D. wrightii*, sacred jimsonweed (pictured at right). Both are found in pastures, waste ground, and agricultural areas, as well as alongside rural roads. They prefer sunny spots, but tolerate some shade.

GROWTH: An erect annual plant, generally 2 to 4 feet tall and bushy, with smooth, **purplish stems that fork repeatedly.** Each fork bears a white or pale lavender flower shaped like a deep, angular funnel with well-defined edges and sharp tips. The flowers have a pleasant scent, but all other parts of the plant have a foul odor, especially when crushed.

LEAVES: Alternate, dark green on top, lighter below; generally 4 to 6 inches long. Thorn-apple leaves have **pointed, irregular teeth and several lobes;** they resemble an elongated maple or red-oak leaf. Sacred jimsonweed leaves typically have **wavy edges and shallow or nonexistent lobes.**

FRUIT: Thorn-apple fruit is egg-shaped, about 2 inches long, growing upright from the fork of the stems. Fruit of sacred jimsonweed is more globe-like, up to 1½ inches, growing from the fork on a drooping stemlet. Fruits of both are **covered in spiny prickles.** Fruits are green when young, eventually turning brown and splitting to scatter seeds.

SEASON: Jimsonweed flowers throughout summer and into fall; fruits develop from the flower remnants throughout the season.

COMPARE: Jimsonweed is very distinctive, especially when it is bearing flowers or fruit; there is nothing that would be confused with it.

NOTES: Thorn apple is non-native; it was first noted in Jamestown, Virginia, during colonial days, when it was responsible for mass poisonings. Although sacred jimsonweed is a native plant, both it and thorn apple are considered pests in agricultural areas; cattle can be poisoned if they graze on the plants. Both contain scopolamine, atropine and hyoscyamine, powerful alkaloids that can cause hallucinations, seizures, various physical difficulties, and, occasionally, death.

green = key identification feature   *combined range

WOODY
VINE

ALTERNATE
COMPOUND
LEAVES

SUMMER

Eastern Poison Ivy

Toxicodendron radicans

HABITAT: This native woody vine grows throughout most of our area, and is found in a variety of habitats. It thrives in moist areas with moderate sun such as road ditches, open woodlands, swampy areas and wetlands, but it may also be found in agricultural fields and sandy areas, along fencelines and on disturbed sites.

GROWTH: A woody perennial vine that climbs trees, fences, posts and anything else it encounters, attaching itself to the supporting structure with **thick, hairy stems** (the hairs are actually aerial roots). Stems are reddish to gray. Eastern poison ivy may also grow as a shrub, or even a ground-hugging plant; it also hybridizes with western poison ivy (pg. 256), a low-growing form.

LEAVES: Three-part leaves grow on the ends of long, pale green petioles (stemlets) attached alternately to the main stem. The stemlet of the middle leaflet is **longer than those of the side leaflets**. Leaflets of eastern poison ivy may be up to **7 inches long**, much larger than those of western poison ivy. Edges have **large, irregular teeth**. Leaves turn yellow to reddish in fall, often with a blotchy appearance.

FRUIT: The round, **ridged** berries are ⅛ to ³⁄₁₆ inch across and green when immature, ripening to yellowish-white. Berries of eastern poison ivy grow from leaf axils in loose clusters; the **clusters are usually large and abundant**. Berries, and all other parts of the plant, are toxic and may cause a painful rash if touched.

SEASON: Green berries are present much of the summer, ripening to yellowish-white in the fall.

COMPARE: Western poison ivy (pg. 256) is a **low-growing plant**, not a vine, with smaller leaves and **fewer berries**. Both are toxic.

NOTES: Eastern poison ivy is included here, in the green section of the book, because its abundant green berries are prominent most of the summer, and pose a threat to inquisitive children. See pg. 256 for more information on poison ivy.

green = key identification feature

Aerial roots on stem

VINING
PLANT

ALTERNATE
LEAVES

LATE SUMMER
THROUGH FALL

Wild Cucumber
–OR– Balsam Apple

Echinocystis lobata

HABITAT: Streambanks, moist thickets and woods, roadsides, swamp edges. Generally found in sunny locations.

GROWTH: A native, non-woody vining plant with coiled tendrils; nodes are sometimes hairy. Grows rapidly, and can reach 25 feet in length.

LEAVES: Alternating leaves, somewhat resembling maple leaves, grow on long petioles (stemlets); each typically has five distinct triangular lobes, but may have as few as three or as many as seven lobes. Leaves are up to 7 inches long and nearly as wide.

FRUIT: A pulpy green berry-like fruit with a firm skin (called a *pepo*), 1 to 2 inches long, roughly egg-shaped, sometimes with blunt ends, grows from the leaf node. The fruit has supple, spiny prickles overall. Eventually the fruit dries out and turns brown, splitting open at the end to disperse its four seeds. The fruit is inedible.

SEASON: Wild cucumber blooms in mid to late summer, producing a profusion of lacy white flowers that may blanket surrounding vegetation; fruits are present from late summer through fall.

COMPARE: Wild grapes (pg. 170) are vining plants with similar leaves, but the fruit is entirely different, resembling the familiar commercial grape. Bur cucumber (*Sicyos angulatus*), which is much less common in our area, has a spiny green fruit that is not egg-shaped but rather has many points, looking something like a small, prickly, three-dimensional star ornament; its leaves have much shallower lobes.

NOTES: The roots of wild cucumber have been used medicinally, to treat ailments ranging from headache, stomach problems, rheumatism and even lovesickness. According to *Native American Ethnobotany* (Daniel E. Moerman; Timber Press), the seeds were used as beads by American Indian peoples.

green = key identification feature

SMALL
WOODY SHRUB

ALTERNATE
LEAVES

LATE SPRING
TO SUMMER

*see below

Gooseberries (green stage)

Ribes spp.

HABITAT: Four native gooseberry species are common in our area: prickly or pasture (*Ribes cynosbati*), Missouri (*R. missouriense*), swamp or smooth (*R. hirtellum*), and northern or Canadian (*R. oxyacanthoides*). Gooseberries inhabit thickets and tangled areas, scrubby shelterbelts, rocky areas, and rich, moist woods, especially those along rivers or ponds.

GROWTH: Gooseberry shrubs are typically 2 to 4 feet high. Stems may be up to 6 feet long; as they grow they tend to arch or sprawl, rooting where they touch the ground to create a new plant crown. Stems may be smooth, bristly or prickly, depending on the species. Most gooseberry shrubs have one to three sharp thorns at leaf nodes.

LEAVES: Attached alternately to the stem by a petiole (stemlet). Each leaf has three to five distinct lobes, resembling a maple leaf with rounded teeth. Leaves are slightly to densely hairy on one or both surfaces, depending on species (see pgs. 174 and 226 for more details about the species).

FRUIT: The ¼- to ½-inch round berry grows singly or in clusters of two or three. Prickly gooseberry fruits have soft prickles, either overall or around the half of the fruit closest to the stem; fruits of the others are smooth. All have distinct stripes running lengthwise; a flower remnant, called a pigtail, is present at the end of the berry. Gooseberries are green when young, ripening to red, purple, or blackish.

SEASON: Fruit is green but edible in late spring through midsummer.

COMPARE: Currant shrubs (pg. 120, 228) resemble gooseberry shrubs, but fruit is borne in long clusters of multiple fruits. Carolina horse nettle (pg. 58) bears toxic green berries on prickly stems, but it is a shorter plant, not a shrub, with leaves that resemble oak, not maple.

NOTES: Green gooseberries are rich in pectin, and are used primarily for jam and jelly. Taste a few before harvesting; they will be sour, but if they are too astringent, let them mature a bit longer before picking. When the fruits ripen (pgs. 174, 226), they are excellent in baked desserts, sauces and other dishes.

green = key identification feature   *combined range

Missouri gooseberry

Prickly gooseberry

TREE

ALTERNATE
LEAVES

MID TO
LATE SUMMER

*see below

Common Pear

Pyrus communis

HABITAT: This is the common orchard pear, which has escaped cultivation and is found in scattered spots in the wild. Pears may be "planted" by anglers, hunters or picnickers who throw out a core after eating a commercial pear, so they are found near boat launches, parks and hiking trails. Pears do best in warm, sunny areas with rich, moist, well-drained soil.

GROWTH: A medium to large tree, with a straight trunk and an open, spreading crown. Unlike orchard pears, which are grafted onto shorter stock to make picking easy, wild pears grow from seed, and tend to be taller than their domestic cousins. The trunk has furrowed grayish bark. Branches are reddish-brown to grayish; most are smooth, with visible gray lenticels (breathing pores), but side branches often have wrinkled bark or are knobby-looking. Pear trees have no thorns.

LEAVES: Glossy, thick, leathery leaves, up to 4 inches long and two-thirds as wide, grow alternately or in clusters on long yellowish-green petioles (stemlets). Leaves have pointed tips and are broadest near the base or below the midpoint; they often fold in slightly along the midline. Edges are finely serrated, and may appear wavy.

FRUIT: A greenish to yellowish pome, generally 1 to 2 inches across; the skin is rough, with fine brown patches or tiny dots. Pears grow on a thick stemlet and have a crown on the bottom. Unlike commercial pears, wild pears have little or no neck; they often grow with the crown end up, looking like a large, rough-skinned greenish crabapple. Wild pears are generally firmer than domestic pears, but taste similar. There are no toxic look-alikes that have a crown on the bottom.

SEASON: Wild pears ripen in mid to late summer.

COMPARE: Crabapples (pg. 162) are similar trees, but leaves taper at both ends, and are thinner and rougher than pear leaves; branches of most crabapples in the wild have thorns.

NOTES: Wild pears may fall off the tree before fully ripe, but will ripen if left on the countertop for a few days.

green = key identification feature   * specific locations not available

48

TREE

ALTERNATE
LEAVES

LATE SUMMER
TO EARLY FALL

Pawpaw
Asimina triloba

HABITAT: Areas with deep, rich soil, including bottomlands, stream and river-banks, floodplains, ravines and ditches. Pawpaw prefers sun, but also grows in shady areas; it produces the most fruit in sunny areas.

GROWTH: This native tree can attain heights up to 40 feet, but is usually much shorter; it may appear shrub-like. It often grows in a "patch" or thicket, with larger central trees towering over the smaller surrounding upstarts. Bark is smooth and light brown, often with light-colored splotches; it has numerous small, wart-like lenticels (breathing pores). Twigs are downy when young, becoming smooth as they mature.

LEAVES: Thick, bright green leaves grow alternately on short petioles (stemlets); they tend to cluster towards the ends of the branches. Leaves are oblong, with tapered bases and a pointed tip; they are up to 11 inches long and about one-third as wide, broadest above the midpoint. They have smooth edges and numerous prominent veins.

FRUIT: Green, smooth-skinned fruits grow singly or in clusters on short, thick stemlets along the branches. Fruits are typically oblong and some-what irregularly shaped; they are 2 to 6 inches long. Ripe fruits are softer to the touch, and are often pale yellowish-green with brown flecks. The interior of the ripe fruit is creamy yellow, with 8 to 13 large, flat, oval inedible seeds. The fruit is a prime edible, tasting similar to a banana with pineapple and apricot overtones (it is often called Indiana banana). It can be eaten raw, or used in baked goods. It may cause stomach upset or intestinal problems in some people. There are no toxic look-alikes.

SEASON: Pawpaw fruits are present much of the summer, but don't ripen until late summer to early fall.

COMPARE: A smaller form, the dwarf or small-flowered pawpaw (*A. parvi-flora*) grows in the southeast but not in our area.

NOTES: Pawpaw fruit is rich in vitamin C, potassium and iron. It was a dietary staple of American Indians and early settlers, and was much favored by the Lewis and Clark expedition members.

green = key identification feature

Leaves

TREE

ALTERNATE LEAVES

FALL

Osage Orange
–OR– Hedge Apple

Maclura pomifera

HABITAT: Open sunny areas and rich bottomlands are prime habitat. It is also found in pastures and along fencerows, and occasionally along riverbanks.

GROWTH: A deciduous tree, up to 40 feet high with approximately equal width. Osage orange has many branches, and the foliage is dense, giving the appearance of a very solid tree. The trunk has brown bark with strong **vertical fissures**. Only female trees bear fruit, and not until they are about 10 years old.

LEAVES: Bright green oblong leaves, 3 to 7 inches long, grow alternately on the stems. Leaves are smooth and glossy, with a rounded base and sharply pointed tip; although the edges are smooth, the leaves tend to curl upwards along the edges and may appear wavy. Half-inch-long thorns grow at each leaf nodule. If a leaf or thorn is pulled off, **milky sap** will appear on the stem (careful; the sap may irritate the skin).

FRUIT: The **pebbly-textured, leathery sphere**, 4 to 6 inches across, consists of a pithy core surrounded by abundant small seeds. The fruit is light green when immature, ripening to yellowish-green with a tinge of orange and a mild orange scent. Osage orange fruit is generally regarded as mildly toxic; sap from the fruit can cause skin irritation.

SEASON: Osage orange blooms in early summer; the large, round fruit grows throughout summer, ripening in fall.

COMPARE: Nothing in our area resembles the fruit of the Osage orange.

NOTES: Osage orange is named after the Osage, an American Indian tribe that inhabited the tree's native range in Oklahoma and portions of the surrounding states. It is not native to our area, having been introduced as a hedge plant. Some people place Osage orange fruits around the foundation of the house, in the basement or near windows and doors to repel insects. The fruit also provides food for squirrels, who shred it and strip the slimy husk off the seeds before eating them.

green = key identification feature

Mature fruit and thorns

TENDER
LEAFY PLANT

OPPOSITE
LEAVES

MID TO
LATE SUMMER

Mayapple –OR– Mandrake

Podophyllum peltatum

HABITAT: Rich, somewhat shaded woodlands with loamy soil. This native plant grows in shade, but requires moderate sun to produce fruit.

GROWTH: A smooth green stem grows from the underground rhizome (root-bearing stem) to a height of 12 to 18 inches; a large palmately lobed leaf grows at the top of the stem. Some plants have a forked stem, with a large leaf on top of each fork; only forked plants will flower and produce fruit. Mayapples usually grow in large colonies.

LEAVES: Each deep green, palmately lobed leaf is 8 to 10 inches wide and has five to nine lobes with toothy edges; the overall outline is a circle. Plants with a single stem have one leaf, while those with a forked stem have two. A colony of mayapple plants resembles a miniature woodland café, with the leaves serving as patio umbrellas.

FRUIT: In spring, a single flower grows on a long stemlet from the fork in the stem. An egg-shaped green berry appears after the flower, and matures slowly over the summer; full-sized berries can be up to 2 inches long. When the leaves start dying, the plant falls to the ground, usually with the unripe green fruit still attached; foragers typically gather the fruit at that time and let it ripen to yellow on the countertop. Fully ripe berries are edible raw but are usually cooked or juiced; they have a lemony, tropical taste, and numerous small seeds like those of cantaloupe. Caution is essential because *unripe berries and all other parts of the plant are toxic*. As with all wild edibles, eat only a small portion until you are sure you won't have an adverse reaction. Before picking or eating any mayapples, it's best to get the guidance of a forager who is experienced in judging ripeness of the fruit.

SEASON: Berries ripen to yellow from mid to late summer.

COMPARE: Goldenseal (pg. 78) has a similar growth habit, with a forked stem topped by a large leaf, but its fruit is a red compound drupe.

NOTES: The rhizome is extremely toxic, but is used medicinally to treat genital warts; studies suggest it may have anti-cancer properties.

green = key identification feature

Unripe mayapple berry on plant (all parts of the plant are toxic at this stage)

Ripe mayapple berry

TENDER
LEAFY PLANT

ALTERNATE
LEAVES

MID TO
LATE SUMMER

*see below

Ground Cherry

Physalis virginiana and others

HABITAT: Fields, slopes and waste ground; often found along fences, streams and railroad grades. The varieties here are native to our area.

GROWTH: A very leafy plant, 1 to 4 feet tall. Depending on variety, it grows as a perennial from **underground rhizomes** (root-bearing stems), or as an annual from a **taproot**. In our area, perennials include the Virginia (*Physalis virginiana*), clammy (*P. heterophylla*) and smooth (*P. longifolia;* also listed as *P. subglabrata*) ground cherry. The downy ground cherry (*P. pubescens*) is an annual; it is fairly uncommon in our area.

LEAVES: Alternate, on short to medium petioles (stemlets). Leaves are generally toothy, although some have smooth edges. Virginia ground cherry leaves are **narrow** and have tapered bases; leaves may be softly hairy or nearly smooth. Smooth ground cherry leaves and stems are **hairless** or nearly so. Leaves of clammy, smooth and downy ground cherry are generally **egg-shaped**. Clammy ground cherry leaves have rounded teeth around the entire leaf, while those of the downy variety are toothed primarily on the upper half; stems of both are densely hairy.

FRUIT: A round, many-seeded berry, ½ to ¾ inch across, is enclosed in a **ribbed husk** that hangs from a leaf axil or stem fork. Berries of Virginia, clammy and downy ground cherries are golden yellow when ripe; those of the smooth ground cherry are orangish to purplish. *Unripe berries and all other parts of the plant, including the papery husk, are toxic.* Ripe berries of the smooth ground cherry should be cooked before eating; ripe berries of the others listed here may be eaten raw or cooked.

SEASON: Yellow bell-shaped flowers, generally with dark spots inside the base, are present all summer; the berries ripen in mid to late summer.

COMPARE: Some nightshades (*Solanum* spp.) have similar husks. If the husk is smaller than ½ inch, is unribbed, or clings tightly to the berry, do not pick the fruit; it is inedible and may be toxic.

NOTES: The related tomatillo, used in Mexican cooking, is similar in form and appearance, but it doesn't grow in the wild in our region.

green = key identification feature   *combined range

Ripe ground cherries

Husks containing unripe ground cherries (all parts of the plant are toxic at this stage)

Clammy ground cherry

Smooth ground cherry

TENDER
LEAFY PLANT

ALTERNATE
LEAVES

SUMMER
THROUGH FALL

Carolina Horse Nettle
Solanum carolinense

HABITAT: Found in pastures, waste ground and disturbed areas; also along roads, fences and railroad grades. Prefers sunny areas.

GROWTH: An erect, branching herbaceous plant that is typically about 2 feet tall, although it can grow to 3 feet. Its hairy stems are armed with sharp spines that can stick in the skin and break off, making it despised by gardeners. It is not native to our area, but has become naturalized.

LEAVES: Alternate, bright green, covered with fine, starry hairs on both surfaces. Leaves are irregularly lobed and shaped like an oak leaf with rounded tips; they are up to 7 inches long and are attached to the stem by short, spiny petioles (stemlets). The midribs and parts of the veins have small but sharp thorns.

FRUIT: A round, many-seeded berry, about 1 inch in diameter at maturity. Fruits are borne in drooping clusters on a leafless stem. Immature berries are bright green with darker, somewhat blotchy stripes. Green fruit is toxic, and is sometimes blamed for cattle deaths. When ripe, the glossy yellow-to-orangish berries resemble small, yellow tomatoes. Ripe berries smell foul and are reported to be toxic in large quantities.

SEASON: White or purple flowers appear in late spring, and continue to appear through late summer. Fruits develop a week or two later, and can be found through early fall.

COMPARE: Buffalobur nightshade (*S. rostratum*) also has sharp spines and thorns, but its leaves have deeply cleft, rounded lobes; its greenish-yellow fruits are covered with long, sharp prickles. It is fairly uncommon in our area but does grow in scattered areas. Carolina horse nettle resembles eastern black nightshade (pg. 216), which has similar flowers, fruits and leaf shape. However, eastern black nightshade does not have spines; its fruits are much smaller, and are black when mature.

NOTES: Despite its common name, horse nettle is a member of the nightshade family, not the nettle family (*Urtica* sp.). It is resistant to herbicides and is considered a noxious agricultural pest.

green = key identification feature

Ripe fruit

TREE

ALTERNATE LEAVES

LATE SUMMER TO EARLY FALL

Russian Olive
– OR– **Oleaster**

Elaeagnus angustifolia

HABITAT: An introduced plant, Russian olive is found in floodplain forests, irrigation ditches, and grasslands. It also grows along railroad grades, roads and fencelines. It tolerates seasonal flooding, but also survives in areas that suffer occasional drought. Prefers sun, but will grow in dappled shade. A very adaptable plant.

GROWTH: A small tree, sometimes appearing as a large shrub; up to 20 feet tall, often with a rounded, spreading crown. Branches are silvery when young, maturing to reddish brown; some have small thorns.

LEAVES: Lance-shaped leaves are grayish-green above; the undersides are silvery. They grow alternately and are generally 2 to 4 inches long and one-quarter as wide, with smooth margins and a well-defined midrib. Leaves are rough-textured on both sides.

FRUIT: The oval drupe, about ½ inch long, is yellow when ripe, and is covered with fine silvery scales. Fruits grow abundantly along the stems from short, scaly stemlets. The fruit, although somewhat dry, is sweet, and can be eaten raw, pulped to make fruit leather, or cooked for jam. It is quite astringent when underripe.

SEASON: Pleasantly scented yellow flowers appear in spring; the fruit follows and ripens in late summer to early fall.

COMPARE: Autumn olive (pg. 146) has a similar silvery appearance, but its leaves are wider, roughly one-half as wide as they are long. Fruits of autumn olive are rounder and smaller, and are red with silvery scales; they are also juicier and sweeter than those of Russian olive.

NOTES: Russian olive was widely planted during the 1800s in disturbed areas; it is good for stabilizing embankments. It also offers cover and food for wildlife. Nonetheless, it is considered invasive in some areas because it shades out native understory plants and spreads rapidly.

green = key identification feature

TENDER
LEAFY PLANT

ALTERNATE
LEAVES

MID TO
LATE SUMMER

False Toadflax
–OR– Northern Comandra

Geocaulon lividum

HABITAT: Moist woods with dappled shade. Also found in peaty bogs and mossy areas. Tolerates poor soil.

GROWTH: An erect native perennial, 4 to 12 inches in height. Stems are generally unbranched. Although it is able to photosynthesize, it also uses suckers (shoots) to attach itself to the roots of other plants, stealing water and nutrients from them; bearberry (pg. 108) and asters are often its chosen hosts.

LEAVES: Oval leaves with blunt tips, ¾ to 1½ inches in length and one-half as wide, grow alternately on the stems from short petioles (stemlets) that flow smoothly into the leaf. Leaves are light green with a dull, almost dusty appearance, and sometimes have yellow streaks, which are caused by a species of rust fungi (lodgepole pine blister rust). They often develop a reddish hue in late summer.

FRUIT: A juicy, bright orange drupe that is typically about ¼ inch across grows from a short stem in the leaf axil. Some sources report it as edible, but not tasty, while others recommend against eating it.

SEASON: Flowers appear all summer; fruits are present from mid to late summer.

COMPARE: False toadflax plants resemble bastard toadflax (pg. 82), but the fruit of bastard toadflax is green with reddish blotches and a long, pinkish or whitish floral crown.

NOTES: Some sources list false toadflax as *Comandra livida*. The plant is somewhat uncommon in our area, and is considered endangered in parts of its range. It was used medicinally by American Indian peoples, who dressed wounds with a poultice made by chewing leaves and stems; the leaves and bark were also used to make a tea that is said to induce vomiting, helping to purge the system.

green = key identification feature

TENDER
LEAFY PLANT

OPPOSITE
LEAVES

LATE SUMMER

*see below

Horse Gentian
–OR– **Feverwort**

Triosteum aurantiacum, T. perfoliatum

HABITAT: Rocky and wooded areas, especially with rich soil; thickets; wooded ridgetops. Prefers areas with dappled sun.

GROWTH: An erect, unbranched native perennial, 2 to 4 feet in height. Stems are covered with fine, long hairs; leaves are slightly hairy on the edges and the undersides.

LEAVES: Large, oval leaves, up to 8 inches long and one-half as wide, grow oppositely in pairs; the edges have no teeth and the leaf terminates in a sharp tip. Leaf pairs grow in intervals along the stem; each pair is rotated 90° from the previous pair. Two varieties inhabit our area; they are distinguished mainly by the leaves. Early horse gentian (*Triosteum aurantiacum,* pictured at right) has leaves that are distinct from one another, and are connected to the stem by a tapering neck. The leaves of perfoliate horse gentian (*T. perfoliatum*) are perfoliate, connected at the base which clasps the stem.

FRUIT: Orange berries, about ⅓ inch in diameter, grow at the leaf axils; typically, three to five berries grow in each axil. Each berry has a small crown of narrow leaves, making the grouping of berries appear spiky. The fruit is inedible and will cause intestinal problems in large quantities, but the seeds of perfoliate horse gentian (sometimes called wild coffee) were sometimes roasted and used as a coffee substitute.

SEASON: Red or purple flowers bloom in early summer, and are followed by oblong green berries, which enlarge and ripen in late summer.

COMPARE: The alternating growth pattern of the leaves, and the flowers clustered in the leaf axils, make horse gentian easy to identify; once the berries develop, this plant can't be confused with any other.

NOTES: Horse gentian attracts bumblebees, who use their long tongues to extract nectar from the long-necked flowers.

green = key identification feature   * combined range

VINING
PLANT

ALTERNATE
LEAVES

LATE SUMMER
THROUGH FALL

American Bittersweet
Celastrus scandens

HABITAT: Found in rich woods, swamp edges, field edges and disturbed areas. Also grows on bluffs and rocky slopes. It grows best and produces more fruit in full sun, but will tolerate light shade.

GROWTH: A native perennial woody vine, bittersweet is often seen climbing on trees, fences and shrubs. It can grow to 30 feet in length. Bark of older stems becomes scaly and corky in appearance.

LEAVES: The glossy, dark green leaves have finely serrated edges and are roughly oval in shape with sharply pointed tips; they are 2 to 4 inches long and about one-half as wide. Leaves grow alternately on the vine, which has a **slightly twisting habit**, sometimes causing the leaves to appear to rotate along the stem. Leaves turn yellow and drop off in fall.

FRUIT: A round berry-like capsule, about ¼ inch across. Small clusters of fruits grow **at the branch tips**; fruits are green when young, ripening to yellowish-orange in late summer. In fall, the capsules split open to reveal seeds with a **shiny, orange-red coating**, making an attractive fall display. The fruits are mildly toxic and should not be eaten.

SEASON: The vine flowers in late spring. Unripe fruits develop in early summer, maturing in late summer and splitting open in fall.

COMPARE: May be confused with Oriental bittersweet (*C. orbiculatus*), an aggressive introduced vine that kills other plants by smothering or girdling them. Young shoots of Oriental bittersweet have **small thorns** that are absent on American bittersweet; leaves of the Oriental variety tend to be **wider, almost round**. The fruits of Oriental bittersweet grow **from the leaf axils** rather than from the branch tips, and the insides of split-open capsules are **yellow**, while those of American bittersweet are **orange**.

NOTES: The capsules remain on the plants through winter, providing food for ruffed grouse, pheasant, quail, rabbit, songbirds and squirrels. Branches containing clusters of the dried, split-open fruits are used to add color to flower arrangements.

green = key identification feature

Oriental bittersweet

Split capsule of
American bittersweet

TREE

ALTERNATE
COMPOUND
LEAVES

LATE SUMMER
THROUGH FALL

*see below

Mountain Ash

Sorbus spp.

HABITAT: Three varieties of mountain ash inhabit our area: the native American mountain ash (*Sorbus americana*) and showy mountain ash (*S. decora*), and the introduced European mountain ash (*S. aucuparia*). All are found on rocky ridges, in sun-dappled woods, and at the edges of forests. They require ample moisture and moderate to full sunlight; American and showy mountain ash are very cold-tolerant.

GROWTH: A small tree, generally no higher than 30 feet, with spreading branches and an open crown. Bark is smooth and brownish with numerous lenticels (breathing pores) when young, turning rough and gray with age.

LEAVES: Compound leaves with 11 to 17 leaflets grow alternately on the stems; leaflets are narrow with serrated edges, and paler below than above. Leaflets of American and showy mountain ash are about **2 inches long, with pointed tips**; the overall leaf is up to 10 inches long. Leaflets of showy mountain ash are **more rounded at the base** and slightly less narrow than those of American mountain ash. European mountain ash leaflets are **1 to 1½ inches long** and **coarsely serrated with blunt tips**; overall leaf is 5 to 8 inches long.

FRUIT: Small pomes, each about ⅜ inch across, grow in dense clusters. Fruits are greenish-white when immature, and ripen to bright orange (American and European varieties) or **deep reddish-orange** (showy). It can be difficult to distinguish between species when confronted with them in the field; fortunately, fruits from all three are edible. The fruit is somewhat astringent, becoming a bit milder after a frost. It is usually used to make jelly, or as a seasoning for meat.

SEASON: Fruits ripen in late summer through fall, and remain on the trees through winter.

COMPARE: Fruiting mountain ash trees resemble nothing else in our area.

NOTES: Mountain ash is an important fall and winter food source for birds including grouse, waxwings and grosbeak, as well as for black bears.

green = key identification feature
* combined range

European mountain ash

TENDER
LEAFY PLANT

ALTERNATE
COMPOUND
LEAVES

EARLY
SUMMER

Ground-Plum Milkvetch
Astragalus crassicarpus

HABITAT: This native perennial grows in open, rocky or gravelly areas, particularly those with limestone content. It is found in rocky meadows and prairie areas, along roadsides, and in sparse, rocky woodlands.

GROWTH: Stems grow from a central crown, and are typically 6 to 12 inches in length, although they may be longer. Stems are fleshy, and covered with fine hairs; they are reddish, or green tinged with red. Young stems are upright, but when fruits develop, the stems usually sprawl on the ground. In late spring, the plants have abundant clusters of pink to purple orchid-like flowers. Ground-plum plants have **no tendrils**.

LEAVES: Compound leaves, 2 to 5 inches in length, grow alternately. Leaves have 7 to 16 pairs of small, narrow, lance-shaped leaflets on the hairy, pale-green leaf stemlet; a terminal leaflet is usually present. Leaflets are pale and dull green in color, with smooth edges; they average ½ inch in length and are about one-quarter as wide. Undersides are hairy; the top sides may be **smooth, or have scattered fine hairs**.

FRUIT: **Plump, smooth-skinned, egg-shaped pods**, about an inch long and containing numerous small black seeds, grow in clusters at the ends of non-leafy stems. Fruits are greenish when immature, ripening to **brickish-red**. They have two lengthwise seams; the bottom of the fruit bears a long, thin tail. *Young* fruits are edible raw, cooked or pickled; care must be taken to ensure proper identification, as some plants with similar leaves and flowers have toxic fruits (see below).

SEASON: Fruits develop in late spring, ripening in early summer.

COMPARE: Other plants with similar leaves and flowers inhabit our area, but their fruits are shaped like **pea pods**, which may be flat or fattened in appearance; some are oval, like a large kidney bean. These include other *Astragalus*; purple locoweed (*Oxytropis lambertii*); and numerous vetches (*Vicia* spp.), which are vining plants **with tendrils**. Many of these pea pod-like or oval fruits are toxic; none should be eaten.

NOTES: Seek advice from a skilled forager before eating ground-plum.

green = key identification feature

TENDER
LEAFY PLANT

WHORLED
LEAVES

SUMMER

*see below

Strawberries

Fragaria spp.

HABITAT: Prefers well-drained soil in full sun to part shade. Often found in rocky areas alongside rural roads, streams and lakes, and in open woodlands, disturbed areas, meadows and fields.

GROWTH: Two types of native wild strawberries inhabit our region: the Virginia or wild strawberry (*Fragaria virginiana*), and the less-common woodland strawberry (*F. vesca*). Both are erect, leafy plants 4 to 8 inches high, with white, 5-petaled flowers. Since both types spread by aboveground runners (horizontal stems, also called stolons), it's not uncommon to find a good-sized patch of wild strawberries.

LEAVES: Coarsely toothed trifoliate leaves grow at the ends of a long, fuzzy stem. The terminal tooth of a woodland strawberry leaf is longer than the surrounding teeth, while it is shorter than the surrounding teeth on a Virginia strawberry, helping distinguish the two varieties.

FRUIT: The heart-shaped strawberry is technically not a fruit; the actual fruits are the darker seeds embedded on the surface of the swollen receptacle (the base of the flower, which is normally inside the fruit). Woodland strawberries are about ½ inch long when mature; the seeds sit on the surface of the receptacle. Virginia strawberries are slightly smaller, and the seeds are slightly embedded in depressions on the surface of the receptacle. Both are rich red when ripe. Strawberries continue to flower throughout summer, so flowers and fruit are present at the same time once the season gets going.

SEASON: Strawberries flower from late spring through midsummer; tiny yellow fruits follow the flowers, swelling and ripening to a juicy red fruit a week or two later. Strawberries often produce fruit all summer.

COMPARE: Dewberries such as the dwarf raspberry (pg. 84) have similar trifoliate leaves, but the dewberry fruit is a compound drupe. Mock strawberries (pg. 90) have upright, round fruits with red seeds.

NOTES: Although smaller than commercial varieties, wild strawberries are sweeter and more intensely flavored, and well worth seeking.

green = key identification feature

* combined range

Virginia strawberry

Woodland strawberry

TENDER
LEAFY PLANT

ALTERNATE
COMPOUND
LEAVES

SUMMER

Red Baneberry

Actaea rubra

HABITAT: This native plant grows in shady areas amid moist hardwoods and mixed forests. Often found in dappled woods alongside bracken fern and large-leaved aster.

GROWTH: Two to four doubly-compound leaves, each up to 15 inches long, grow alternately on the main stem. The total height is 1 to 2½ feet. Flowers grow on a separate, leafless stalk that branches off one of the leaf stalks; the flowers generally rise above the surrounding leaves.

LEAVES: Three large compound leaflets grow on each of the long leaf stalks attached to the main stem; each has three or five smooth, sharply toothed leaflets oppositely attached by short stalks. The terminal leaflet is often slightly larger than side leaflets.

FRUIT: Firm, glossy berries about ⅜ inch long, slightly oval to round with a shallow vertical groove. Each berry has a small black dot at the bottom. Berries are typically red, although sometimes they are white. Berries grow in a loose cluster at the top of the thin flower stalk, and are attached to the stalk by thin, green stemlets. The berries are toxic.

SEASON: Ripe berries can be seen from early through late summer.

COMPARE: The related white baneberry (pg. 254) has similar leaves, but the flower stalk and stemlets are thick and knobby, usually reddish-pink, while those of the red baneberry are green and thin; the dot on the bottom of the berry is larger on white baneberries. Berry color is not always an accurate indicator of species, since red baneberry sometimes has white berries; the appearance of the flower stalk is a reliable indicator. Jack-in-the-pulpit (pg. 94) has a tight cluster of red berries, but it has two thick stems, each with a large three-part leaf.

NOTES: All parts of the plant should be considered toxic; contact with leaves may cause skin irritation in sensitive individuals. Ingestion of the berries may lead to dizziness, vomiting or cardiac arrest. Birds eat the berries with no ill effect, helping disperse the seeds.

green = key identification feature

Red baneberry
with white berries

TENDER
LEAFY PLANT

WHORLED
LEAVES

SUMMER

*see below

Trilliums

Trillium spp.

HABITAT: Three native red-fruited trillium grow in our area: nodding trillium (*Trillium cernuum*), bent trillium (*T. flexipes*; also called drooping trillium) and purple trillium (*T. erectum*; also called red trillium). All three inhabit rich deciduous or mixed forests with ample moisture and moderate to heavy shade.

GROWTH: A single stem has a whorl of three broadly oval leaves at the top. The flower grows on a stalk that emanates from the center of the leaf whorl. After blooming, the sepals dry out but remain on the plant during fruit development. All three are generally about 12 inches in height, but can grow taller in good conditions.

LEAVES: Roughly oval, with smooth edges, deep veins and sharply pointed tips. Leaf length and shape help distinguish the three species. Purple trillium leaves are 2 to 7 inches long and roughly as wide; nodding trillium, 2 to 6 inches long and slightly wider than long; bent trillium, 4 to 10 inches long and roughly as wide.

FRUIT: The three trillium species listed here have berry-like capsules with sharply defined edges; each has three internal chambers containing seeds surrounded by wet pulp. The fruit helps distinguish the species. Fruits of nodding trillium are deep pink or red and about 1 inch across on a long stalk that curves down so the fruit is tucked under the leaves. Bent and purple trillium fruits sit above the leaves on a long stalk. Fruits of bent trillium are ¾ to 1½ inches across and pinkish-red, while those of purple trillium are ⅜ to ⅝ inch across and purplish-red to deep red.

SEASON: Trillium flowers in the spring; fruits ripen in midsummer.

COMPARE: Several trillium species in our area have similar growth habits, but fruits are greenish when ripe. White or large-flowered trillium (*T. grandiflorum*) is the most common; its fruits are about ½ inch across.

NOTES: Some trillium fruits are edible, while others are considered toxic. However, the plants are protected in many locations and fruits should not be disturbed.

green = key identification feature

* combined range

Nodding trillium

White trillium fruit

Purple trillium fruit

TENDER
LEAFY PLANT

ALTERNATE
LEAVES

SUMMER

Goldenseal

Hydrastis canadensis

HABITAT: This native plant grows in moist, shady deciduous woods, on slopes, in ravines and along forest edges. It prefers loamy soil that is rich with organic matter, and is often found in seasonally flooded areas.

GROWTH: A fuzzy stem grows from the yellowish rhizome (an underground root-bearing stem) to a height of 6 to 18 inches; a large palmately lobed leaf grows at the top of the stem. Some plants have a forked stem, with a leaf on top of each fork; only forked plants will flower and produce fruit. Goldenseal usually grows in large colonies.

LEAVES: The flowering/fruiting plant has two palmately lobed leaves. One leaf is usually larger, up to 9 inches in length, with almost equal width; a smaller leaf bears the fruit atop a short stemlet. Each leaf has three to seven lobes with toothy edges. Leaves are hairy on both surfaces, and are sometimes very wrinkly.

FRUIT: Ripe goldenseal fruit is a red, compound drupe about ½ inch across that somewhat resembles a red raspberry (pg. 116). Individual drupes of goldenseal are somewhat pointed, whereas the drupes of raspberries are rounded and more closely joined. The fruits are mildly toxic and should not be eaten.

SEASON: Fruit is green in late spring, ripening to red in summer.

COMPARE: Mayapple (pg. 54) has a similar growth habit, with a forked stem topped by a large leaf; however, its fruit is a 2-inch berry that is yellowish when ripe. Red raspberries (pg. 116) somewhat resemble goldenseal fruit, but raspberries grow as an arching, thorny bramble.

NOTES: Goldenseal (particularly the rhizome) contains the alkaloids berberine, hydrastine and canadine, and has been used medicinally since pre-Colonial times. It has been used to treat everything from cancer, poor appetite, and diarrhea to fever, stomach problems, ringworm and earache. It has recently come into use as an augment for the immune system. Overharvesting and habitat loss have endangered native stocks of the plant, and it is now listed as an endangered species.

green = key identification feature

TENDER
LEAFY PLANT

ALTERNATE
LEAVES

SUMMER

Rose Twisted Stalk

Streptopus lanceolatus

HABITAT: This native plant prefers coniferous and hardwood forests with cool, rich soil and ample moisture. It is common in the southern part of the boreal forest.

GROWTH: The arching, hairy stem grows from an underground rhizome (root-bearing stem). The stem bends slightly at each leaf axil, giving it a zigzag appearance. Total length is 1 to 2 feet.

LEAVES: Lance-shaped leaves with deep parallel veins grow alternately on the stem. Each leaf is 2 to 4 inches long and about one-half as wide, with a rounded base and a sharp tip; edges and the veins on the underside have fine hairs. Leaves of rose twisted stalk are sessile (attached directly to the stem); those of a very similar species, clasping-leaved twisted stalk (*S. amplexifolius*) clasp the stem.

FRUIT: Juicy red berries, about ½ inch long and slightly narrower, grow singly or in pairs at the leaf axils. Berries hang below the leaves, on a thin stemlet that has a bend in it. Twisted stalk berries are mildly toxic but can be eaten in small quantities. Eating more than a few will cause diarrhea; this gives rise to the nickname "scoot berry," which is sometimes applied to the fruit. It's best to consider them inedible.

SEASON: Rose twisted stalk develops pinkish flowers in late spring; those of clasping-leaved twisted stalk are white to greenish-yellow. Berries replace the flowers and ripen in midsummer.

COMPARE: Several plants have similar leaves and growth habit, but are easy to distinguish. Common false Solomon's seal (pg. 36) and starry false Solomon's seal (pg. 38) bear fruits at the end of the stem. Smooth Solomon's seal (pg. 184) is much larger, and it bears blue fruits at the leaf axils. Large-flowered bellwort (pg. 34) has perfoliate leaves, and each stem bears a single triangular-shaped fruit.

NOTES: Rose twisted stalk is sometimes called rose mandarin; clasping-leaved twisted stalk is then referred to as white mandarin. Rose twisted stalk is listed in some texts as *S. roseus*.

green = key identification feature

TENDER
LEAFY PLANT

ALTERNATE
LEAVES

MID TO
LATE SUMMER

Bastard Toadflax
–OR– **Comandra**

Comandra umbellata

HABITAT: This native plant is found in meadows, grasslands, prairies, edges, and dry, open woods; occasionally found in mixed evergreen forests. It requires plenty of sunlight and good drainage.

GROWTH: This small, erect perennial is typically 4 to 8 inches high, but can reach 12 inches; it often grows in large colonies. Stems are light green and smooth, and woody near the base. Although it is able to photosynthesize, it also uses suckers (shoots) to attach itself to the roots of other plants, stealing water and nutrients from them.

LEAVES: The thick, alternate leaves are 1 to 2 inches long and about one-quarter as wide. They are attached directly to the stem or by a very short petiole (stemlet). Leaves are light grayish-green and smooth, with smooth edges. Some leaf tips may have a slight reddish tinge. The midvein is prominent on the underside of the leaf.

FRUIT: A green drupe about ¼ inch across, with reddish blotches and a long, pinkish or whitish floral crown at the end; the fruit seems large in proportion to the plant. The fruits are sweet when young, but have thin flesh with a slightly oily texture. They make an acceptable trailside nibble, but are not worth seeking out. Later in the season, the fruits darken, finally becoming brown and unappetizing.

SEASON: Bastard toadflax produces white flowers in late spring through midsummer; fruits ripen in mid to late summer.

COMPARE: The leaves and growth habit of bastard toadflax resemble true toadflax (*Linaria* spp.), but *Linaria* don't produce drupes. False toadflax (pg. 62) is similar, but ripe fruits are bright orange and have no crown.

NOTES: The flower stamens have small hairs at their bases, giving the plant its species name, *Comandra* (a combination of the Greek words for "hair" and "man"). *Umbellata* refers to the flat-topped, umbrella-like flower clusters.

green = key identification feature

TENDER
LEAFY PLANT

ALTERNATE
COMPOUND
LEAVES

MID TO
LATE SUMMER

Dewberries

Rubus pubescens and others

HABITAT: Numerous varieties of dewberries inhabit our region; most are native and the differences between species are fairly subtle. The most common red-fruited dewberry is *Rubus pubescens*, often called the dwarf red raspberry. Dewberries prefer rich, moist forests, ranging from the boreal forests of the far north to mixed or hardwood forests of the south. They inhabit the same areas as the related red raspberry (pg. 116) and black raspberry (pg. 222), sprawling beneath their taller kin.

GROWTH: A low plant with erect leaves, found **creeping along the ground in vine-like fashion**. Stems are usually smooth or slightly hairy, although some dewberries, referred to as bristle-berries, have bristly stems.

LEAVES: Coarsely toothed trifoliate leaves with a **sharply pointed tip** grow alternately on the trailing stem. Leaflets are smooth to somewhat hairy. The compound leaf can be up to 4 inches long, but is usually shorter.

FRUIT: The compound drupe, ¼ to ½ inch across, resembles a raspberry; however, the dewberry's receptacle (core) **usually remains inside the picked fruit.** Ripe dewberries range from rich red, as shown in the photo at right, to purple, to black. All are edible and sweet, although quality and taste varies among the numerous varieties and from one plant to another.

SEASON: Dewberries ripen from mid to late summer.

COMPARE: Many dewberries (pg. 232) have fruits that are **black** when ripe. Wild strawberry (pg. 72) has similar trifoliate leaves, but the fruit is **not a compound drupe**; strawberry leaflets have **blunt tips**. Red and black raspberries (pgs. 116, 222) have similar leaves, but grow as **arching brambles several feet long**; fruits are **hollow** when picked. Goldenseal (pg. 78) has similar-looking fruits, but the leaves resemble **large maple leaves**; goldenseal fruits are mildly toxic and should never be eaten.

NOTES: If you find red dewberries that are hard and dry, they may be unripe specimens of a variety that ripens to purple or black. Let them ripen until soft, regardless of color, before harvesting.

green = key identification feature

TENDER
LEAFY PLANT

WHORLED
LEAVES

MID TO
LATE SUMMER

Bunchberry

Cornus canadensis

HABITAT: This native plant inhabits cool, shady coniferous and mixed-wood forests; it is sometimes found in boggy or swampy areas. Abundant in the boreal forest.

GROWTH: Technically a shrub, bunchberry grows as a leafy plant that is typically 4 to 8 inches high. It grows from a spreading underground rhizome (root-bearing stem) and is often found in a large colony.

LEAVES: Each plant has one or two groupings of four to six leaves that grow oppositely; pairs grow so closely spaced on the stem that the leaf groups have a **whorled appearance**. The deep green, shiny leaves are oval, with pointed ends and deep veins that curve from base to tip; they are typically 1 to 3 inches in length, and about three-quarters as wide. A flower stalk rises from the center of the top leaf pair.

FRUIT: Round, bright red drupes, ¼ inch across, grow in a **cluster from the flower stalk at the top of the plant**. The fruits are edible, but mealy and bland, and are not worth seeking out. They can be eaten raw as a trail nibble, added to fruit salads for a bit of color, or cooked into jam, jelly, sauce or pudding. Bunchberry is a good survival food to know about.

SEASON: Tiny greenish flowers with large white bracts (leaves borne on a floral axis) appear from late spring through early summer; the flowers develop into fruits, which ripen in mid to late summer.

COMPARE: Canada mayflower (pg. 252) has leaves that somewhat resemble those of bunchberry, but Canada mayflower has only **one to three leaves** per plant, and its veins are **much less pronounced**. (A leaf of Canada mayflower is visible in the photo at right, just above the sliver of white wood to the right of the top bunchberry plant.)

NOTES: Bunchberries have a unique pollination method; when the closed flower is touched, it opens explosively—in less than a millisecond—to release its pollen, throwing it up to an inch away at a speed of 10 feet per second (according to a study reported in a 2005 edition of the journal *Nature*).

green = key identification feature

TENDER
LEAFY PLANT

ALTERNATE
LEAVES

MID TO
LATE SUMMER

Asparagus

Asparagus officinalis

HABITAT: This non-native plant is found in sunny pastures and fields, along roadsides and railroad grades, in ditches and on embankments. It is most common near agricultural areas, where it has escaped cultivation.

GROWTH: Asparagus is a commonly grown vegetable that develops into a bushy, multi-stemmed fern-like plant with **feathery, drooping fronds**. It can grow up to 6 feet in height, with equal width. In mid to late summer, small red berries develop on the fronds.

LEAVES: The true leaves are actually **small scales on the main stem**; they are the same as the dark, dagger-like leaves on the stalk of the familiar asparagus shoot. The wispy, fern-like appearance of the plant comes from branches with soft, needle-like leaves; the branches grow alternately on the main stem.

FRUIT: Round red berries, about ¼ inch across or slightly larger, grow on thin, bent stemlets from the upper wispy branches. The berries contain toxins and should not be eaten.

SEASON: Asparagus shoots develop into the "asparagus fern" by early summer. Berries ripen to red by mid to late summer.

COMPARE: Asparagus is easy to identify at all stages. At a distance, the fern stage of the plant may resemble any number of overgrown leafy plants, but close inspection of an asparagus plant, with its scale-like leaves on the stalks, will confirm its identity. Check the base of the plant; you'll see the asparagus spears you're familiar with, but the pointy top has grown into the fern-like stems. You may even be able to see last year's withered, browned stalks (see small photo at right). Remember the location, and come back the following spring to harvest fresh, wild-grown asparagus spears.

NOTES: Wild asparagus is simply the cultivated vegetable that has escaped the farm or garden. Birds eat the red berries, and the wild plants are often found near farms that grow asparagus.

green = key identification feature

Close-up of base

Asparagus plant in "fern" stage

TENDER
LEAFY PLANT

ALTERNATE
COMPOUND
LEAVES

MID TO
LATE SUMMER

Mock Strawberry
–OR– Indian Strawberry

Potentilla indica

HABITAT: Originally from Asia, mock strawberry is sometimes planted as an ornamental, and has escaped cultivation to become a pest in many areas. It is found in parks, lawns, open woodlands, fields and waste ground, growing best in partial shade.

GROWTH: A low-growing plant that creeps along in vine-like fashion. The trailing stem is hairy, and green to purplish-green; it roots at leaf nodes, often forming large, mat-like colonies. Individual stems may be a foot or more in length.

LEAVES: Three-part compound leaves grow alternately on long, hairy green petioles (stemlets). The oval leaflets have rounded teeth around the entire edge; they are up to 2½ inches in length and two-thirds as wide. Leaflets are smooth on the top surface; underneath, the veins are hairy.

FRUIT: A soft, fleshy red globe whose surface is covered with raised red seeds, the mock strawberry looks like a round, red-seeded version of the familiar strawberry. Mock strawberry fruits grow upright on a hairy stem that arises from the leaf axils; green bracts (leaf-like structures) grow around the base of the fruit. The interior is pale pinkish-white. Although edible, mock strawberries are almost tasteless, and the faint flavor they do have is mildly unpleasant.

SEASON: Yellow flowers appear in profusion from late spring through mid-summer; fruits are ripe from mid to late summer.

COMPARE: True strawberries (pg. 72) look similar, but the seeds on the surface are dark; leaves are toothed only on the top half, while the lower half of the leaf is smooth-edged. True strawberries have white or pale pink flowers.

NOTES: Some references list this plant as *Duchesnea indica*. It spreads easily and is likely to become more common in the wild. The name, Indian strawberry, is a reference to the plant's Asian origins.

green = key identification feature

Typical colony

TENDER
LEAFY PLANT

COMPOUND
LEAVES

LATE SUMMER
TO FALL

American Ginseng

Panax quinquefolius

HABITAT: Rich, moist hardwood forests and ravines; often found on north-facing slopes. This native plant prefers shade or dappled sunlight.

GROWTH: A smooth green stalk grows from the underground rhizome (root-bearing stem), with a whorl of compound leaves at the top. A separate, long flowering stalk rises from the joining point of the leaves. The total height of the plant is 12 to 18 inches.

LEAVES: Ginseng plants typically have three compound leaves, although there can be as many as five leaves per plant. Each leaf is on a long stalk. Leaves are typically five-parted and about 10 inches across; individual leaflets are roughly oval in shape, with a short stalk, pointed tips, toothy edges and a pronounced midvein. The length of individual leaflets ranges from 3 to 8 inches; frequently, the two leaflets closest to the center of the plant are much smaller than the others.

FRUIT: A cluster of shiny red berries grows on a long stalk from the center of the plant; berries are a flattened oval. The berries are inedible.

SEASON: Ginseng flowers in early to mid summer. Berries ripen in late summer to early fall.

COMPARE: The leaves of ginseng resemble those of five-leaved ivy (pg. 188), but five-leaved ivy is a vine, its berries are blue, and its leaf edges are more coarsely toothed. Sarsaparilla (pg. 212) has a cluster of compound leaves, but the fruiting stalk grows separately from the leaf stalk and is topped with black berries. The bright red berry cluster of ginseng may be mistaken for that of Jack-in-the-pulpit (pg. 94), but Jack has two compound leaves that are three-parted, the stems are thick and purplish, and the red fruit is an oblong cluster 1 to 3 inches tall on a thick stalk that grows from the juncture of the leaf stalks.

NOTES: Ginseng is highly valued for its rhizome, which has medicinal properties. Overharvesting of the wild plants has severely depleted native stocks; now, most ginseng is grown commercially and the wild plant is considered endangered in most of its range.

green = key identification feature

TENDER
LEAFY PLANT

OPPOSITE
LEAVES

LATE SUMMER
TO FALL

Jack-in-the-Pulpit

Arisaema triphyllum

HABITAT: Sun-dappled deciduous forests with adequate moisture.

GROWTH: An erect, native perennial 1 to 3 feet in height that grows from a thick tuber. Each plant has one or two compound leaves that grow at the top of long, thick stalks which are purplish-green. The flower is quite distinctive. A tubular green sheath (called a spathe), with purple or white stripes, surrounds the clublike structure (called a spadix) that bears the actual flowers at its top; the spathe extends over the spadix at the top, forming a hood. The spathe can be up to 6 inches tall; the enclosed spadix is typically 2 to 3 inches in height.

LEAVES: A three-part leaf sits atop each long leaf stalk; leaflets are up to 6 inches long and broadly oval, with a sharply pointed tip. Leaflets are joined directly to the leaf stalk, with no petiole (stemlet). Leaves usually have died back or fallen over by the time the fruit is ripe.

FRUIT: An elongated, tightly joined cluster of shiny berries develops from the spadix; ripe berries are bright red. Individual berries are about ⅜ inch across; the cluster is 1 to 3 inches in height and about one-third as wide. The berries are mildly toxic and should not be eaten.

SEASON: Plants flower from mid spring to early summer. Green fruit follows shortly after, ripening to bright red in late summer to early fall.

COMPARE: The ripe red fruit cluster resembles that of several other plants, but the leaves help distinguish them. Red baneberry (pg. 74) has several doubly-compound leaves and looks lacy in comparison to Jack. Wild calla (pg. 96) grows only in very wet areas and has several thick stalks, each with a simple leaf. American ginseng (pg. 92) has three or more five-part compound leaves. Green dragon (*A. dracontium*; in our area, found primarily in the southern parts of Wisconsin and Michigan) has a compound leaf with a wishbone- or arc-shaped stem that joins the stalk at its center; each leaf has 7 to 15 unevenly sized leaflets.

NOTES: All parts of the plant contain calcium oxalate crystals, which cause an intense burning sensation if eaten.

green = key identification feature

Green dragon leaf

Ripe fruit

TENDER
LEAFY PLANT

BASAL
LEAF GROWTH

LATE SUMMER
TO FALL

Wild Calla –OR– **Water Arum**

Calla palustris

HABITAT: Bogs, swamps, marshes, ponds and other wet areas; often found in marshy shores next to rivers, streams and lakes. This native plant is found both in shallow water and along the edges of wet areas.

GROWTH: Several large leaves grow from the underground rhizome (root-bearing stem). In late spring, the plant produces a showy flower-bearing structure that looks like a bumpy yellow club (called a spadix), 1 to 2 inches long, next to a furled white sail (called a spathe) about 2 inches in height; the entire structure rises about 6 inches above the water on a stalk. The actual flowers are carried by the spadix, and are insignificant in appearance.

LEAVES: Glossy, bright green heart-shaped leaves grow on long, thick stalks. Leaves are typically 5 or 6 inches in length; stems can be up to 12 inches long. The base of the leaf is rounded, and deeply notched where it joins the stalk.

FRUIT: The small flowers on the spadix turn into pear-shaped berries that are bright red when ripe, leading to what looks like a bright red, bumpy club rising from the center of the leaves. The fruit is inedible and generally regarded as mildly toxic when fresh, although when dried and ground, both the berries and rhizome are edible.

SEASON: The flowering structure is present from late spring through summer; the fruit cluster ripens in late summer to early fall.

COMPARE: The ripe red fruit cluster resembles that of Jack-in-the-pulpit (pg. 94), which grows in forested areas and has two large three-part compound leaves at the tops of long, thin stalks.

NOTES: Wild calla is often fertilized by snails that crawl along the spadix. All parts of the plant contain calcium oxalate crystals, which cause an intense burning sensation if eaten when fresh.

green = key identification feature

Fruit

TENDER
LEAFY PLANT

OPPOSITE
LEAVES

LATE SUMMER
THROUGH FALL

Partridge Berry
–OR– Two-Eyed Berry

Mitchella repens

HABITAT: Deciduous and mixed-wood forests with rich, acidic soil; also found in bogs, along streambanks and in areas with sphagnum moss. The plant tolerates dry to moist soil.

GROWTH: A creeping, ground-hugging native plant that roots at the leaf nodes, spreading to form a low mat on the forest floor. It is typically 2 inches in height or less.

LEAVES: Rounded, glossy, deep green leaves, broad at the base and tapering to a rounded point, grow opposite one another on the long, trailing stem. Leaves are ½ to ¾ inch in length and slightly less wide; they are attached to the stem with short petioles (stemlets). The midrib is thick and lighter in color; undersides are yellowish. Leaf edges are smooth.

FRUIT: The smooth drupe, about ¼ inch across, has two small dimples or depressions, formed when the paired flower buds grow together. This gives rise to the common name "two-eyed berry." The fruit is red when ripe; there are no toxic look-alikes because the two "eyes" are very distinctive. The drupe is edible but not particularly tasty, and is not worth seeking out; it makes an acceptable trail nibble or survival food.

SEASON: Partridge berry produces white to pale pink flowers in early summer; the flowers are followed by the fruit, which ripens in late summer and may persist over winter if not eaten by birds.

COMPARE: Cranberry (three species, pg. 106), bearberry (pg. 108) and creeping wintergreen (pg. 110) are small trailing plants like partridge berry, but leaves on these other plants are alternate, not oppositely attached like leaves of partridge berry.

NOTES: The genus is named after Dr. John Mitchell, an eighteenth-century botanist and physician from Philadelphia. Partridge berry is used by modern-day herbalists as a tonic.

green = key identification feature

Closeup

VINING
PLANT

ALTERNATE
LEAVES

SUMMER
TO FALL

Climbing Nightshade

Solanum dulcamara

HABITAT: Moist hardwood forests and thickets, swampy areas, waste ground, roadsides and streambanks. Climbing nightshade prefers partial shade and abundant moisture.

GROWTH: A sprawling, non-native vine that produces many slim, scraggly branches that climb over other plants. It can appear as a short plant, but often grows to 10 feet in length, occasionally even longer. Branches are green or purplish, and often hairy, when young, turning brownish-green, smooth and woody as they mature; the base of the plant is woody. Flowers are **bright purple with yellow centers**. All parts of the plant have an unpleasant scent when crushed.

LEAVES: Bright green, shiny, heart-shaped leaves grow alternately on the branches; many leaves have **two ear-like lobes at the base**. The petioles (stemlets) are slightly flattened. Overall leaf length is up to 3 inches; the ear-like lobes span a width of up to 2 inches.

FRUIT: The glossy, many-seeded berry is up to ½ inch long and usually slightly narrower, although it can also be round rather than egg-shaped. Berries are green when immature, turning orange and finally **bright red** when ripe. All parts of the plant, including the berries, are highly toxic.

SEASON: Berries are produced throughout summer and into fall, remaining on the plant even after the leaves have fallen off.

COMPARE: Eastern black nightshade (pg. 216) has similar fruits, but it has tiny **white** flowers and its berries are **black** when ripe; leaves lack the lobes at the base, and the plant is a **tender perennial** that is only **1 to 3 feet** in height.

NOTES: This plant is also called woody nightshade or bittersweet nightshade, a reference to the bittersweet compound dulcamarine which is found in all parts of the plant, but especially the roots. It also contains solanine, a toxic alkaloid found in the green parts of the common Irish potato (*S. tuberosum*) and other members of the nightshade family.

green = key identification feature

VINING
PLANT

OPPOSITE
LEAVES

LATE SUMMER
THROUGH FALL

Twining Honeysuckle

Lonicera dioica

HABITAT: Dry, open hardwood or mixed-wood forests and thickets; rocky areas; clearings.

GROWTH: A climbing, native woody vine, up to 10 feet in length. Young stems have a waxy bloom, and are green or sometimes purplish-red; older stems are brown or gray and often have shreddy bark.

LEAVES: Smooth, oval leaves with rounded tips grow oppositely, attached directly to the stem or by a short petiole (stemlet); leaves are 1½ to 4½ inches long, and about one-half as wide, and the edges are hairless. One or more pairs of leaves at the end of the stem are joined at the bases to form a cup around the stem. Flowers grow in a cluster on a short stalk at the center of the terminal cup; they develop into fruit clusters.

FRUIT: Smooth, reddish oval berries, about ⅜ inch long, grow in a cluster from the center of the terminal leaf cup. The berries are very bitter, and should not be eaten.

SEASON: Red flowers are present from late spring through midsummer. The berries ripen from late summer through early fall.

COMPARE: A related species, hairy honeysuckle (*L. hirsuta*) has leaves that are rough and slightly hairy, with hairy edges; young stems are also hairy and lack the waxy coating. Other characteristics of the two plants are extremely similar. In our area, hairy honeysuckle is found only in the northern half. Grape honeysuckle (*L. reticulata*) is a climbing woody vine with similar growth habit and fruits, but its leaves are broader—almost round—and stems are grooved; in our area, it is found in scattered locations in southern Wisconsin and the far southeastern tip of Minnesota.

NOTES: Twining honeysuckle is sometimes called limber honeysuckle or red honeysuckle; the latter name comes from the color of the flowers and fruit. Birds eat the seeds, helping to propagate the plant.

green = key identification feature

VINING
SUBSHRUB

OPPOSITE
LEAVES

LATE SUMMER
TO FALL

Running Strawberry-Bush
Euonymus obovatus

HABITAT: This native plant is found in areas with rich, well-drained soil including thickets, woodlands and swamp edges. It prefers shade or dappled sunlight, and is often found on north-facing slopes.

GROWTH: A **ground-hugging, trailing plant**, it is technically a subshrub, but vine-like in growth habit. Young stems are smooth and bright green, becoming purplish or brown with age; they are thin and flexible, and often **develop roots where they contact the ground.** Running strawberry-bush frequently grows in **large, mat-like colonies**; the plants are generally 12 inches or less in height, but individual stems can grow to several feet long as they sprawl on the ground.

LEAVES: Oval to egg-shaped leaves, broadest at or above the mid-point with a tapered base and roundly pointed tip, grow oppositely on short petioles (stemlets) that are sometimes grooved. Leaves are smooth and bright green, 1½ to 2½ inches in length and half to two-thirds as wide; edges have fine teeth. In fall, the leaves turn purplish or pink.

FRUIT: The most distinctive part of the plant. A **warty-looking, rounded capsule,** about ¾ inch across and slightly flattened, grows on a thin stem-let from a leaf node. The capsule is white at first, turning pink or orange and eventually **splitting into three parts to reveal two to four seeds with bright red, fleshy coating.** The fruits are inedible.

SEASON: Fruit capsules develop from greenish flowers in early summer; the capsules are white in midsummer, turning pink and splitting open in late summer to early fall.

COMPARE: Winged euonymus (pg. 150) is related, but it is a non-native plant that grows as a **large woody shrub** rather than a vine-like sub-shrub. Eastern wahoo is another related plant that grows as a large shrub; for more detail, see pg. 150.

NOTES: The fruits are eaten by wild birds; the leaves are browsed by deer and rabbits.

green = key identification feature

Ripe fruit

VINING
SUBSHRUB

ALTERNATE
LEAVES

LATE SUMMER
THROUGH FALL

*see below

Cranberries

Vaccinium spp.

HABITAT: Three species of wild cranberry are native to our region: small cranberry (*Vaccinium oxycoccus*), large cranberry (*V. macrocarpon*) and northern mountain cranberry (*V. vitis-idaea* var. *minus*). All are found in wet, acidic areas such as sphagnum bogs, swampy spots and fens.

GROWTH: A ground-hugging trailing plant; technically a subshrub, but vine-like in growth habit. Stems are slender and hairless. Cranberry plants often take root at the leaf nodes, forming dense mats.

LEAVES: Smooth, hairless, leathery evergreen leaves grow alternately on the slender stems. Leaves of small cranberry are less than ⅜ inch long, lance-shaped with pointed tips, and white underneath; edges are rolled. Leaves of large cranberry are ¼ to ⅝ inch long, narrowly oval with blunt tips, and pale underneath, but not as white as those of small cranberry; edges are flat or very slightly rolled. Leaves of northern mountain cranberry are ¼ to ¾ inch long, egg-shaped with rounded tips; undersides have tiny black resin dots (visible with a lens).

FRUIT: A tart, but delicious, red berry. Fruits of northern mountain cranberry and small cranberry grow on stalks at the tip of the stem; those of large cranberry grow along the stem rather than at the tip. Large cranberry has the largest fruits, averaging ½ inch across; those of the other two species are ⅜ inch or less. The fruits of large cranberry look out of proportion to the tiny leaves. There are no toxic look-alikes.

SEASON: Cranberries ripen in late summer to early fall, and may persist on the evergreen plants through winter if not eaten by birds.

COMPARE: Several plants with edible berries have similar appearance. Creeping snowberry (pg. 258) has white berries; stems and leaves are hairy. Creeping wintergreen (pg. 110) has larger leaves, up to 2 inches. Both creeping snowberry and wintergreen smell spicy when crushed. Bearberry (pg. 108) has larger leaves, up to 1 inch, which are pointed at the base and broadly rounded at the tip.

NOTES: Cranberries are best when cooked, but can be eaten raw.

green = key identification feature

* combined range

Northern mountain cranberry

Large cranberry

VINING
SUBSHRUB

ALTERNATE
LEAVES

LATE SUMMER
THROUGH FALL

Bearberry -or- Kinnikinnick *Arctostaphylos uva-ursi*

HABITAT: Sandy or rocky areas in cool, open woodlands; forest and trail edges that are sunny and well drained; elevated shorelines.

GROWTH: A ground-hugging trailing plant, bearberry is technically a sub-shrub, but vine-like in growth habit. This native plant is often seen in a large, mat-like colony. Older stems can reach 3 feet in length; individual shoots rise up to 6 inches tall. Stems are flexible and reddish-brown; the thin bark is often shreddy on older stems.

LEAVES: Leathery, shiny, hairless evergreen leaves grow alternately on short petioles (stemlets); top sides are dark green and the undersides are medium green. Leaves are oval or paddle-shaped, broadest toward the tip, ⅜ to 1 inch in length and one-half as wide; edges are smooth and there is a noticeable fold at the midrib.

FRUIT: A glossy, round berry, about ⅓ inch in diameter, with a dimple at the bottom. Fruit is bright red when ripe. Bearberry is edible, but is mealy and not particularly flavorful. There are no toxic look-alikes.

SEASON: Fruits appear in late summer, ripening throughout late summer and fall. They may persist over winter if not eaten by wildlife.

COMPARE: Several plants with edible berries have a similar appearance. Creeping snowberry (pg. 258) has white berries; its stems and leaves are hairy and the leaves are tiny. Creeping wintergreen (pg. 110) has larger leaves, up to 2 inches. Both creeping snowberry and wintergreen smell spicy when crushed. Cranberry (three species, pg. 106) have smaller leaves that are much lighter underneath. Partridge berry (pg. 98) has red berries, but the leaves grow oppositely rather than alternately.

NOTES: Bearberry leaves have been used medicinally, by American Indian peoples as well as physicians in Europe, to treat conditions including problems with the bladder, kidneys and urinary tract. The berries are a winter food source for bears and grouse.

green = key identification feature

VINING
SUBSHRUB

ALTERNATE
LEAVES

FALL

Creeping Wintergreen
–OR– **Teaberry**

Gaultheria procumbens

HABITAT: This native plant is found in coniferous and mixed-wood forests and clearings, especially areas with moss and peat. Wintergreen prefers moist conditions and light shade, and will grow in sandy areas as well as sphagnum bogs, rocky windswept heights, and swamp edges.

GROWTH: A ground-hugging, trailing plant, it is technically a subshrub, but vine-like in growth habit. It spreads slowly, and may grow as a small cluster, or as a larger colony. Individual shoots are less than 6 inches in height. All parts of the plant have a minty smell when crushed.

LEAVES: Leathery, shiny, hairless evergreen leaves grow alternately on short petioles (stemlets). Leaves are oval, broadest at or beyond the midpoint, with a tapered base and a roundly pointed tip; they are 1 to 2 inches in length and two-thirds as wide. Edges are smooth, and the midrib is light in color.

FRUIT: A glossy, bright red berry, ¼ to ⅓ inch long, with a star-shaped depression on the bottom. The berry is edible but mealy in texture, with a mild wintergreen taste; it makes a decent trail nibble. There are no toxic look-alikes.

SEASON: Berries ripen in early fall, and will remain on the plant through winter unless eaten by wildlife.

COMPARE: Several plants with edible berries have a similar appearance. Cranberry (three species, pg. 106), bearberry (pg. 108) and partridge berry (pg. 98) are small trailing plants like creeping wintergreen, but their leaves are smaller and they don't have a minty smell. Note that partridge berry leaves are oppositely attached, while the others mentioned here are alternately attached.

NOTES: Leaves are often steeped to make a refreshing tea. Upland birds including quail, grouse and pheasant eat the berries; deer browse on the entire plant.

green = key identification feature

SMALL
WOODY SHRUB

OPPOSITE
LEAVES

SUMMER

Canada Fly Honeysuckle

Lonicera canadensis

HABITAT: This native plant is found primarily in the northern part of our range (and also in the northeast U.S.); it grows in a variety of forest types, from the boreal forest and mixed hardwood stands, to swampy thickets. Prefers moderate sunlight; shrubs in shady areas may not bear fruit.

GROWTH: An erect, somewhat straggly shrub, 3 to 5 feet in height and almost as wide. Branches are greenish to purplish and smooth when young, turning gray or brown and developing shreddy bark with age.

LEAVES: Opposite, on short petioles (stemlets); 1 to 3 inches long. Bright green on top, lighter underneath, with smooth edges that are **fringed with fine hairs.** Young leaves have slightly hairy surfaces, while older leaves are smooth. Leaves taper to a slightly rounded point; the bases are tapered on small leaves and rounded on larger leaves.

FRUIT: **Paired oblong red berries are connected at the base,** and grow on a **long stalk** arising from the leaf axil. Berries taper to a **rounded point;** each berry is ¼ to ⅜ inch in length. Canada fly honeysuckle are generally not prolific fruit producers; the berries are noticeable due to their bright color, not their profusion. The berries are not edible.

SEASON: Fruits are present from early summer through late summer.

COMPARE: Swamp fly honeysuckle (pg. 122) has much **narrower** leaves that **lack the hairy fringe** on the edge; its berries are **round** rather than oblong. Bush honeysuckles are easily distinguished from Canada fly honeysuckle; please see the text on pg. 140 for more information about these non-native plants.

NOTES: A few sources report that the berries of Canada fly honeysuckle are edible; most regard them as mildly toxic. Unlike the bush honeysuckles on pg. 140, Canada fly honeysuckle is a native plant.

green = key identification feature

SMALL
WOODY SHRUB

ALTERNATE
LEAVES

SUMMER

Fragrant Sumac
–OR– Skunkbush

Rhus aromatica

HABITAT: Relatively dry areas, including rocky slopes, high streambanks, sand dunes and old pastures. Also found along rural roads and on waste ground. It prefers sun, but will tolerate light shade.

GROWTH: A spreading shrub that is generally 6 feet or less in height; may spread up to 10 feet in width. Twigs are smooth and brown, hairy when young but with no thorns or bristles; numerous branches usually rise above the mound of base foliage. *Rhus aromatica* is native to our area; however, hybrids are frequently planted in landscaping, and may be seen as non-native escapees in our area.

LEAVES: Glossy three-part leaves with scalloped edges grow alternately on long petioles (stemlets). Leaves are 4 to 6 inches long, dark green on top and lighter underneath. The end leaflet is joined directly to the two side leaflets by a long, tapering neck; it is generally larger than the side leaflets. When crushed, the leaves and stems have a noticeable scent which ranges, on individual plants, from pleasant to mildly skunky.

FRUIT: The distinctive hairy, red to reddish-orange drupes grow in clusters at the ends of the twigs. Individual drupes are about ¼ inch in length and slightly less wide. The drupes are lemony-sour and can be used to make a lemonade-type beverage. There are no toxic look-alikes.

SEASON: Fruits ripen in midsummer, and may persist through winter.

COMPARE: Poison ivy (pgs. 42, 256) has three-part leaves that often have scalloped edges, but it has small ribbed berries that are greenish or white; also, the terminal leaflet of poison ivy has a long petiole.

NOTES: Although fragrant sumac is not a major wildlife food source, deer occasionally browse on the foliage and twigs; small mammals and birds eat the fruits, particularly in winter. The fruits were reportedly salted and eaten by pioneers. Some references list this plant as *R. trilobata*, a reference to the three-part leaves.

green = key identification feature

SMALL
WOODY SHRUB

ALTERNATE
COMPOUND
LEAVES

SUMMER

Red Raspberry

Rubus idaeus

HABITAT: Open woods, thickets, edges; one of the first plants to appear in an area that has been cleared or burned. Some red raspberries found in the wild are native, while others are descendents of cultivated plants.

GROWTH: Red raspberries are brambles, sprawling vine-like shrubs that often form a thicket. Stems, called canes, grow to 5 feet in length, and are usually arching but may also be upright. Canes are prickly but have no thorns. Young canes are reddish or greenish in color; older canes are brownish and shreddy.

LEAVES: Compound, doubly-toothed leaves with sharply pointed tips grow alternately on the canes; undersides are pale. Leaves usually have three to five leaflets, occasionally seven; they are up to 8 inches long. The terminal leaflet has a short petiole (stemlet), while the side leaflets are attached directly to the stem.

FRUIT: A compound drupe, up to ½ inch across and usually equal in length. Fruits are green and hard at first, turning pinkish and finally ripening to rich red. Ripe fruits detach cleanly from the plant, leaving the receptacle (core) behind; the picked fruit is hollow.

SEASON: Red raspberries ripen in midsummer, generally after black raspberries and well before blackberries.

COMPARE: Underripe black raspberries (pg. 222) resemble red raspberries, but canes have large, heavy thorns and a whitish bloom. Goldenseal (pg. 78) has similar fruits, but leaves resemble large maple leaves; goldenseal fruits are mildly toxic and should not be eaten. Dewberries (pg. 84, 232) are low-growing plants with three-part compound leaves and smooth stems; fruits do not detach easily from the receptacle. Thimbleberries (pg. 118) have large maple-like leaves, and the fruit is wider. Blackberries (pg. 234) have similar fruits that are black when ripe; when red, they are hard and dry because they are underripe.

NOTES: One of the easiest wild berries to pick; it's easy to identify, widespread, plentiful and delicious.

green = key identification feature

SMALL
WOODY SHRUB

ALTERNATE
LEAVES

MID TO
LATE SUMMER

Thimbleberry

· Rubus parviflorus

HABITAT: Openings in mixed-wood forests, along rural roads, edges and clearings. Produces more fruit in sunny areas with good moisture, but will tolerate some shade and somewhat dry soil.

GROWTH: An erect, leafy native shrub, 2 to 3 feet tall with equal spread, that often grows in large, open colonies. Older stems are reddish or gray, with shreddy bark; young stems are hairy. There are no thorns or prickles anywhere on the plant. Flowers are white.

LEAVES: Large, light green leaves that resemble wrinkled maple leaves; 4 to 8 inches long and wide. Leaves have three to five pointed lobes, with coarsely toothy edges all around; they grow alternately on long petioles (stemlets). Undersides are paler and may be slightly hairy.

FRUIT: A compound drupe, ½ to ¾ inch across and fairly flat. Fruits are white and hard at first, turning pinkish and finally ripening to rich red; ripe fruits are very soft and juicy. Ripe fruits detach cleanly from the plant, leaving the receptacle (core) behind; the picked fruit is hollow, but so soft that it may crumble upon picking. Although seedy, ripe fruits are usually delicious, with a slight acidic tang that balances the sweetness; thimbleberry is well worth seeking out. Fruit quality varies from plant to plant.

SEASON: Fruits appear on the plants in early summer, and ripen in mid to late summer; typically, thimbleberries are beginning to ripen at the height of the red raspberry season, and continue to ripen after the raspberries are finished.

COMPARE: Purple-flowering raspberry (*R. odoratus*) is up to 6 feet tall, with pinkish to purplish flowers; in our area, it is found primarily in a few counties in eastern Michigan and the Upper Peninsula. Please also see pg. 116 for information on other fruits that resemble thimbleberries.

NOTES: Here's one plant that will never be commercialized; the ripe fruit is so soft that it falls apart easily, making it hard to pick and transport. Use a bucket to hold your harvest of thimbleberries, and don't fill it too deeply or the fruit on the bottom will be crushed.

green = key identification feature

Thimbleberry

Purple-flowering raspberry

SMALL
WOODY SHRUB

ALTERNATE
LEAVES

MID TO
LATE SUMMER

*see below

Red Currants

Ribes spp.

HABITAT: Three varieties of red currant inhabit our region: the non-native garden red currant (*Ribes rubrum*, pictured at right), swamp red currant (*R. triste*; native) and skunk currant (*R. glandulosum*; native). All inhabit cool, moist woodlands, swampy areas, clearings and streambanks.

GROWTH: A straggling shrub, generally about 3 feet in height; garden red currant can reach **5 feet in height**. Stems are smooth and **thornless**; older branches are woody. Garden red currant tends grow in an **upright manner**, while swamp red currant and skunk currant often sprawl along the ground.

LEAVES: Attached alternately to the stem by a medium to long petiole (stemlet). Each leaf has three to five distinct lobes, resembling a maple leaf with rounded teeth. Leaves are 2 to 5 inches long; swamp red currant leaves are usually **slightly hairy below**, while the other two are usually smooth. Leaves of skunk currant have a **disagreeable, skunk-like odor when crushed**.

FRUIT: Round ¼- to ⅜-inch berries grow in **racemes** (long clusters of multiple fruits). Immature berries are green, turning **red** and are somewhat translucent when ripe. All red currants listed here are edible; there are no toxic look-alikes. Berries of garden red and swamp red currant are smooth and glossy, and are tart but delicious when used in baking, or cooked into jelly, jam and other dishes. Berries of skunk currant are **covered with glands and hairs**; some people find them unpalatable.

SEASON: Red currants ripen in mid to late summer.

COMPARE: Black currants (pg. 228) are similar, but berries are **black** when ripe. Gooseberries (pgs. 46, 174, 226) have similar leaves and growth habits, but most gooseberries have **thorns** at the leaf nodes. Gooseberry fruits grow in **clusters of two or three**, in contrast to currant fruits, which grow in a raceme.

NOTES: If you find a currant with red berries, but the berries are hard and opaque, you may have found unripe black currants (pg. 228).

green = key identification feature   * combined range

SMALL
WOODY SHRUB

OPPOSITE
LEAVES

LATE
SUMMER

Swamp Fly Honeysuckle   *Lonicera oblongifolia*

HABITAT: This native plant prefers cool, moist, coniferous areas with a rocky base, especially areas with limestone. Also found along marsh edges and on streambanks. Often grows in the same areas as cedar trees.

GROWTH: A small, open shrub, generally 3 feet high or less. Branches are greenish to purplish and smooth or lightly hairy when young, turning gray and developing shreddy bark with age.

LEAVES: Opposite, with short petioles (stemlets); up to 2½ inches in length and less than one-half as wide. Leaves taper at the base; tips are rounded or softly pointed. Young leaves may have fine down; older leaves are hairless. Undersides are lighter in color than top sides; leaf edges are smooth and hairless.

FRUIT: Translucent round berries are paired, although one of the pair may be so small as to be almost unnoticeable. Berries are at the end of a stalk that grows from the leaf axil; the pair of berries is sometimes joined at the base. Ripe berries are orange, red, or reddish-purple, and about ¼ inch across. The berries are inedible.

SEASON: Light yellow flowers appear in early to midsummer; fruits ripen in late summer.

COMPARE: Canada fly honeysuckle (pg. 112) has much wider leaves, with a hairy fringe on the edge; its berries are oblong rather than round. Mountain fly honeysuckle (pg. 194) grows in the same areas and looks similar to swamp fly honeysuckle, but it has blue berries and hairy leaves. Canada fly honeysuckle is easily distinguished from the various bush honeysuckles; see the text on pg. 140 for more information about these non-native plants.

NOTES: Swamp fly honeysuckle is a native plant, unlike the bush honeysuckles on pg. 140. It is uncommon, found only in the states that border Canada or the Great Lakes, from Minnesota eastward to the Atlantic.

green = key identification feature

SMALL
WOODY SHRUB

ALTERNATE
COMPOUND
LEAVES

LATE SUMMER
TO EARLY FALL

*see below

Rose Hips

Rosa spp.

HABITAT: At least 18 species of roses—some native, others non-native—grow in the wild in our area. They grow in clearings, thickets and open forests; on waste ground; and along lakes, streams and rivers.

GROWTH: A bushy, multi-stemmed shrub, typically 1 to 4 feet in height, with equal spread; sometimes grows as a bramble (a vine-like shrub with arching branches). Stems are armed with **thorns or prickles**, which may be scattered or may blanket the stem thickly. Bark of larger stems is shiny and typically reddish-brown; smaller stems are green.

LEAVES: Compound leaves, each with 3 to 11 oval leaflets, grow alternately. Leaflets are bright green above, and typically have fine hairs on the underside; edges are sharply toothed. The compound leaf is typically between 2 to 4 inches long, usually slightly less wide.

FRUIT: The fruits, called hips, develop at the base of the flower; specific characteristics are quite variable. They range in shape from round to oval; ripe hips are typically red, but they are sometimes orange. Hips always have a group of **withered sepals at the end of the fleshy swelling.** All hips are edible, but they are filled with small, hard seeds that are quite bitter. The best hips for eating have a higher flesh-to-seed ratio. There are no toxic look-alikes.

SEASON: Roses bloom from late spring through summer; hips develop afterwards, and are hard and green most of the summer, ripening in late summer to early fall. They typically persist through winter, and become softer and sweeter after a frost.

COMPARE: Roses are easy to identify, especially when hips are present; no other plant compares to a rose.

NOTES: Rose hips are rich in nutrients, particularly vitamin C. They may be eaten raw or cooked; split the hips and scrape out the bitter seeds and irritating hairs before eating. Palatability varies between species and also from plant to plant. Rose hips are often dried and brewed for tea. Cooked rose hip purée can be used in baked goods.

green = key identification feature   * combined range

SMALL
WOODY SHRUB

ALTERNATE
LEAVES

LATE SUMMER
TO EARLY FALL

Canada Yew

Taxus canadensis

HABITAT: Shady, cool sites in coniferous or mixed-wood forests. Also found along streambanks, edges of bogs and swamps, and other moist, shady areas. Found in old-growth forests, rather than new growth.

GROWTH: A native, bushy evergreen shrub, up to 5 feet in height but usually shorter. Branches grow thickly in an upright spray. The bark of larger stems is reddish; older stems may have large, grayish scales. Yew plants are unisexual—a plant is either male or female, and each produces a different type of flower. Only female plants bear fruit.

LEAVES: Flat, dark green evergreen leaves with sharp tips grow thickly on soft green twigs. The leaves are attached singly in a spiral pattern, but are bent at the bases so they appear to grow in a flat plane from the twig. Leaves are up to 1 inch in length, and less than ⅛ inch wide.

FRUIT: A soft, bright reddish-orange cup called an aril surrounds a single seed; the aril is about ½ inch wide. Yew arils can be eaten by humans, but the seed and all other parts of the plant are dangerously toxic. It's not worth taking the risk; leave the aril alone, and let the birds eat the fruits (birds won't be harmed by eating the seeds).

SEASON: Fruits are green, hard and small in midsummer, swelling and ripening in late summer to early fall.

COMPARE: A cultivated yew species, Japanese yew (*T. cuspidata*), has the same distinctive fruit and very similar leaves, but it typically grows as a tree; in our area, it is found occasionally in Michigan.

NOTES: All parts of yew except the aril (seed cup) contain taxanes, highly poisonous alkaloids which are toxic to humans and most animals. Deer, however, are not affected by the alkaloids, and browse extensively on the leaves; in some areas, yew have become scarce due to deer depredation. Birds eat the seeds contained in the aril, but are not harmed because the seeds pass through before the protective seed coat is dissolved.

green = key identification feature

SMALL
WOODY SHRUB

ALTERNATE
LEAVES

LATE SUMMER
TO EARLY FALL

Japanese Barberry
Berberis thunbergii

HABITAT: This is a cultivated plant that has escaped into the wild; it is drought-tolerant, and highly adaptable. It is often found on the fringes of urban areas, in moist to dry areas. Also grows in open hardwood or mixed-wood forests, pastures, disturbed areas and meadows.

GROWTH: A dense, rounded shrub with arching branches that often extend beyond the mass of the shrub; 3 to 6 feet in height and slightly wider. Leaf nodes have a **sharp thorn**, about ½ inch long. The thin, reddish stems are grooved, and **zigzag** slightly at leaf nodes.

LEAVES: **Paddle-shaped**, broadest near the tip with a tapering base; deep green, with **smooth edges** and a deeply cleft midvein. Leaves are ½ to 1 inch long, and about one-half as wide, and grow in **clusters of two to six**; the clusters alternate along the stem.

FRUIT: Oblong, shiny berries grow on a long stalk from the leaf nodes; the berries are usually abundant. Berries are up to ½ inch in length, and sometimes so narrow that they appear **cylindrical**. They are yellowish-green when immature, ripening to opaque scarlet. The berries are dry, with a sharp, sour flavor.

SEASON: Berries ripen in late summer to early fall. The red berries often remain on the plant through winter, after the leaves have dropped, making this a showy landscape plant.

COMPARE: European barberry (*B. vulgaris*) has a similar growth habit, and may be encountered in our region as a garden escapee. The berries grow in **racemes** (long clusters); leaf edges are **toothy**. Fruits of European barberry are a bit more palatable than those of Japanese barberry.

NOTES: Japanese barberry was introduced as an ornamental in the late 1800s; it has escaped cultivation and often crowds out native plants. It also alters soil chemistry by raising the pH level; this often causes native plants to suffer. Birds consume the prolific berries, spreading the plant; it is considered invasive in most areas in which it appears. Dried berries are used in Mideastern cooking.

green = key identification feature

Thorns and unripe fruit

Ripe fruit

LARGE
WOODY SHRUB

ALTERNATE
LEAVES
(TYP.)

SUMMER

Glossy Buckthorn

Frangula alnus

HABITAT: Open woods, wetlands, abandoned fields. Also found along roads, on the edges of power line cuts, next to ponds and streams, and along paths. Tends to form thickets.

GROWTH: This non-native plant is a large, multi-stemmed shrub up to 20 feet in height; it sometimes appears to be a small tree. Branches often droop down over paths, making the colorful fruits very obvious. Twigs are reddish-brown with fine hairs. The bark is smooth and grayish-brown, with noticeable lenticels (breathing pores) that are slightly raised.

LEAVES: Typically alternate, but may be opposite; smooth edges. Deep green above, lighter and slightly hairy below, with deep veins that form a V at the midrib, then curve near the edges to follow the contour of the leaf. Leaves are oblong with a pointed tip, 2 to 4 inches long and one-half as wide, widest at the midpoint or slightly toward the tip. Leaves turn yellow in fall, and usually remain on the plant longer than leaves of other shrubs or trees in the area.

FRUIT: The ¼-inch berries grow in the leaf axils; often seen as a pair, but may also be single or in small groups. The berries are green with a small dot at the base when they first appear, developing a red blush and then changing to mottled red before ripening to black. They are listed here, in the red section of this book, because they are so frequently seen in the red stage. The berries are mildly toxic and should not be eaten.

SEASON: Fruits are on the plant from early through late summer. Green, red and black fruits may all be present on the plant at the same time.

COMPARE: Common buckthorn (pg. 244) has opposite, toothy leaves that are more rounded. Alder-leaved buckthorn (pg. 236) is 3 feet or less; leaves are finely toothed. Pin cherry (pg. 156) has fruits that resemble those of glossy buckthorn, but the leaves are sharply pointed and toothy.

NOTES: This species was brought to the U.S. as an ornamental in the 1800s. It is considered invasive due to its tendency to spread rapidly, crowding out native plants. Also called European buckthorn and *Rhamnus frangula*.

green = key identification feature

130

Green with red blush

Ripe black fruit

LARGE
WOODY SHRUB

OPPOSITE
COMPOUND
LEAVES

SUMMER

Red Elderberry

Sambucus racemosa

HABITAT: This native plant is common along habitat edges: roadsides, forest borders, shorelines and fencerows. It requires cool habitat; in the southern part of its range, it inhabits moist areas with dappled shade.

GROWTH: A large, fast-growing shrub, sometimes appearing as a small tree. Up to 20 feet in height, but also found much shorter. Bark of older stems is gray to reddish-brown, and covered with numerous warty lenticels (breathing pores). Younger stems are soft and pithy, and often covered with downy hairs.

LEAVES: Compound leaves, each with **5 to 7 leaflets**, grow oppositely on the stem; leaves are 6 to 10 inches long and nearly as wide. Leaflets are 2 to 5 inches long and one-third as wide, oval with a rounded base and pointed tip; edges are sharply toothed. Top sides are dark green and smooth, undersides are paler and may be downy.

FRUIT: Round drupes, about ⅛ inch across, with two seeds, grow profusely in **upright, rounded clusters** atop stalks that rise from the leaf axils; fruits are **bright red** when ripe. The fruits are rank in flavor and somewhat toxic, especially when raw; cooking may render the fruit—but not the seeds—edible, but opinions vary. Leaves, stems and all other parts of all elderberry species are toxic.

SEASON: Berries ripen in early to mid summer, well before those of the common elderberry (see below).

COMPARE: Common elderberry (pg. 176) has similar growth habits, but ripe fruits are **purplish-black**, and grow in **flat-topped** clusters rather than the rounded clusters of red elderberry; common elderberry leaves have **5 to 11 leaflets**. Fruits of common elderberry are edible when cooked.

NOTES: Red elderberry is one of the first shrubs to flower in the spring. The fruits are eaten by many species of birds.

green = key identification feature

LARGE
WOODY SHRUB

OPPOSITE
LEAVES

MID TO
LATE SUMMER

Russet Buffaloberry
Shepherdia canadensis

HABITAT: Open, mixed-wood forests and thickets; streambanks; sandy bottomlands. This native plant does best in moist, rocky areas but it will tolerate drought. Grows in sun or shade; tolerates extreme cold.

GROWTH: A medium shrub with an open form, typically up to 6 feet in height but occasionally taller. Young twigs are covered with small brown and silver scales. Bark of older branches is brownish-red, dotted with orange, and occasionally fissured. Buffaloberry is generally unisexual—a plant is either male or female, and each produces a different type of flower. Fruits are borne on the female plants.

LEAVES: Elliptic, with a rounded tip, smooth edges and slightly tapering base; 1 to 2 inches long and one-half as wide. Tops are green and covered with short, silvery scales, giving the plant a powdery appearance. Undersides have small brown and silver scales similar to those on the twigs. The leaves are somewhat thick, and grow oppositely.

FRUIT: Oval, bright red berries, dotted with fine silver scales, grow on very short stalks at the leaf axils of female plants; berries are about ⅓ inch long. The berries have a small, star-shaped crown at the tip. They are edible but very bitter.

SEASON: Berries ripen in mid to late summer.

COMPARE: A related species, silver buffaloberry (*S. argentea*), is very similar in appearance, but the stems are thorny; its berries are sweeter. Silver buffaloberry is a western plant, found scattered in our area in western Minnesota. Autumn olive (pg. 146) has similar scales on the fruit, twigs and leaves, but its leaves are alternate and much longer.

NOTES: Russet buffaloberries contain saponin, a bitter substance that may cause intestinal upset. Saponin foams in water, giving the plant its common nickname, soapberry. American Indian peoples in British Columbia still make a traditional dessert that takes advantage of this foaming property, mixing buffaloberries with raspberries or other sweet fruit, then beating the mixture into a bittersweet froth.

green = key identification feature

LARGE
WOODY SHRUB

ALTERNATE
LEAVES

LATE
SUMMER

Common Chokecherry

Prunus virginiana

HABITAT: Mixed-woods or hardwood forests, clearings, parklands, slopes, river and creek embankments. Tolerates dry, sunny conditions.

GROWTH: A large native shrub, up to 25 feet in height but usually much shorter. Generally open in form and somewhat straggly. Bark is reddish-brown to gray and is smooth, with visible lenticels (breathing pores); smaller stems are often reddish. Shrubs frequently form thickets.

LEAVES: Broadly oval, smooth leaves grow alternately on petioles (stemlets) that are often reddish. Leaves are dark green above, paler underneath; edges are finely toothed. Leaves are 2 to 4 inches long, roughly one-half as wide, tapering at or beyond the middle of the leaf to a broad point. The petiole has several small glands (visible with a lens).

FRUIT: Shiny round drupes, ⅜ inch across, grow in racemes (long clusters of multiple fruits). Fruits are green and hard when immature, ripening to red to reddish-purple, and sometimes blackish; when ripe, they are soft and somewhat translucent. Each drupe contains a single egg-shaped pit which is fairly large in proportion to the amount of flesh. Chokecherries have a delicious sweet-tart flavor, although they are quite astringent when eaten raw. There are no toxic look-alikes.

SEASON: Chokecherries ripen in late summer.

COMPARE: Black cherries (pg. 248) have similar long clusters of fruits, but the leaves are much narrower and have reddish hairs along the midrib on the underside. Pin cherries (pg. 156) have narrower leaves; fruits grow in small clusters, each on its own stem, rather than racemes. Serviceberries (pg. 178) have similar leaves, but the fruit is a pome, an apple-like fruit with a crown; serviceberry fruits are not translucent.

NOTES: Chokecherry leaves and pits contain hydrocyanic acid, a cyanide-producing compound. The leaves and pits should never be eaten, and care should be taken to avoid crushing chokecherry pits when juicing the fruits. Cooking or drying eliminates the harmful compound.

green = key identification feature

Chokecherry bark

NOT EDIBLE

LARGE
WOODY SHRUB

ALTERNATE
COMPOUND
LEAVES

LATE
SUMMER

Prickly Ash
–OR– Toothache Tree
Zanthoxylum americanum

HABITAT: Moist, sun-dappled hardwood and mixed-wood forests; river bottoms, ravines and thickets; bluffs and rocky hillsides.

GROWTH: A thorny, multi-stemmed native shrub, typically 8 to 10 feet in height; occasionally grows as a small tree, up to 25 feet high. Bark is brown or gray; twigs are reddish-brown with white spots. Bark sometimes splits, revealing yellowish wood. Stems are armed with thorns that are up to ½ inch long. All parts of the plant have a citrus fragrance.

LEAVES: Compound leaves, up to 10 inches long, with five to 11 leaflets, grow alternately. Leaflets are oval, ¾ to 3 inches long and one-half as wide, with broad bases and softly rounded tips; dull green above, paler below. The terminal leaflet is on a petiole (stemlet) that is typically short; all others attach directly to the greenish stem.

FRUIT: Rounded, berry-like fruits grow in clusters along the stems. Fruits are reddish to orangish at maturity, and have a bumpy texture. They are technically follicles, dry capsules containing seeds; they split open when ripe to release the shiny black seeds. The fruits are inedible, but in the past they were reportedly chewed to relieve toothache. According to *The Dictionary of Useful Plants* (Nelson Coon; Rodale Press), the seeds may be cooked and used as a pepper substitute.

SEASON: Fruits ripen in late summer, splitting open to release their seeds (one or two per follicle) by summer's end.

COMPARE: There are no confusing look-alikes. Leaves resemble those of the locust family (*Robinia* spp.) but locusts bear fruits that are flat and pod-like. The unusual fruits of prickly ash make this plant unmistakable when it is bearing fruit.

NOTES: The flowers, which are inconspicuous and appear in spring, are attractive to bees. The fruits are eaten by wildlife, including vireo and other birds, rabbits and chipmunks.

green = key identification feature

LARGE
WOODY SHRUB

OPPOSITE
LEAVES

SUMMER
THROUGH FALL

*see below

Bush Honeysuckles

Lonicera spp.

HABITAT: Five types of non-native bush honeysuckle with red or orange-red berries inhabit our region: Amur (*Lonicera maackii*), Tatarian (*L. tatarica*), Morrow's (*L. morrowii*), European fly (*L. xylosteum*) and showy bush honeysuckle (*L. × bella*). All are considered invasive. They inhabit forest edges, parklands and shelterbelts. Highly adaptable, they prefer full sun with ample moisture, but tolerate shade and moderately dry soil.

GROWTH: Multi-stemmed shrubs with spreading crowns. Amur honeysuckle is the largest, up to 15 feet high with equal spread. Tatarian honeysuckle is up to 10 feet high and wide; European fly, 8 to 10 feet high and wide; Morrow's and showy bush honeysuckle, up to 8 feet high and wide. Bark on older branches is often shreddy, peeling off in vertical strips.

LEAVES: Opposite, oval leaves, 1 to 2½ inches long, with short petioles (stemlets). Amur leaves are shiny and dark green, with a sharply pointed tip. Morrow's and showy bush honeysuckle are blue-green and slightly hairy underneath; tips are rounded. Tatarian honeysuckle's leaves are blue-green and smooth, with a tip that is pointed but not as sharp as Amur's. European fly's leaves are grayish-green and hairy.

FRUIT: A juicy, round berry, ¼ inch in size; most are red when ripe, but berries of Morrow's and Tatarian are sometimes orange even when ripe. Berries often grow in pairs and may appear to be joined at the base, but each berry is distinctly round. Morrow's and Amur honeysuckle berries have a ½-inch stemlet; the berry stemlet is very short on the other three listed here. Fruits of all non-native honeysuckles are bitter and inedible.

SEASON: Bush honeysuckles are one of the first plants to develop leaves in the spring. Ripe berries are present from summer through fall.

COMPARE: Canada fly honeysuckle (pg. 112) is typically 3 to 5 feet high; leaf margins are hairy, and the red paired fruits are pointed at the tips. Swamp fly honeysuckle (pg. 122) is usually about 2 to 3 feet high; leaves are narrow and tapered. Both of these are native species.

NOTES: Birds devour honeysuckle berries, propagating the plants.

green = key identification feature

* combined range

Amur honeysuckle

Tatarian honeysuckle

Morrow's honeysuckle

LARGE
WOODY SHRUB

OPPOSITE
LEAVES

LATE SUMMER
TO EARLY FALL

Highbush Cranberry *Viburnum opulus* var. *americanum*

HABITAT: Moist, sun-dappled mixed-wood forests and thickets; swampy areas; river valleys and streambanks; edges and clearings. This native plant thrives in full sun, but can tolerate a fair amount of shade.

GROWTH: A deciduous, multi-stemmed shrub with a rounded crown, up to 15 feet high with equal spread. Bark is smooth and grayish-brown.

LEAVES: Three-lobed, maple-like leaves with fine, sparse hairs on the top attach oppositely to the stems on grooved petioles (stemlets). Leaves are typically 2 to 5 inches in length, slightly less wide. Lobes are sharply pointed, typically with a few small teeth on each lobe.

FRUIT: Shiny, reddish-orange drupes grow in large, showy clusters. Individual drupes are ¼ to ½ inch long and slightly narrower. Fruit clusters grow on a long, reddish stem, and may droop slightly with the weight of the fruit. Ripe, soft fruits of highbush cranberry are tart and astringent but edible, with a taste similar to commercial cranberries; they are usually used for making jelly, jam or sauce. There are no toxic look-alikes.

SEASON: Fruits ripen in late summer to early fall.

COMPARE: Guelder rose or European cranberrybush (*V. opulus* var. *opulus*) is a related, introduced species that appears very similar. The best way to distinguish them is to examine the tiny glands (visible with a lens) at the base of the leaf stalk. The tips of the glands on guelder rose are noticeably concave, but convex or dome-shaped on highbush cranberry. Guelder rose leaves also lack hairs on top. Fruits of guelder rose are very bitter, and have a foul smell when cooking; most foragers consider them inedible. Mapleleaf viburnum (pg. 242) has similar leaves, but it is a shorter plant and its ripe fruits are egg-shaped and black. Thimbleberry (pg. 118) has large, maple-like leaves, but is a much shorter plant; its fruits are compound drupes.

NOTES: Highbush cranberries aren't related to true cranberries (pg. 106), but they taste similar, giving the plant its common name. Older references list this plant as *V. trilobum*.

green = key identification feature

Highbush cranberry

Guelder rose

LARGE
WOODY SHRUB

ALTERNATE
LEAVES

LATE SUMMER
TO EARLY FALL

Winterberry

Ilex verticillata

HABITAT: Moist to wet areas including mixed-wood forests, thickets, and swampy and boggy areas. Plants in full sun produce more fruits.

GROWTH: An erect native shrub up to 15 feet in height, although usually shorter; it tends to produce multiple suckers (shoots), and is often found in large clumps. Bark on mature stems is dark gray to brown, smooth, and mottled with pale lenticels (breathing pores). Smaller stems are purplish-brown. Winterberry is generally unisexual—a plant is either male or female, and each produces a different type of flower.

LEAVES: Elliptical leaves are attached alternately to the stems on petioles (stemlets) that are typically purplish-red. The leaf veins are prominent. Both ends of the leaf taper; leaves are 2 to 4 inches long and about one-third as wide. Edges of the leaf are sharply toothed, especially on the top two-thirds. Leaves are glossy and bluish-green, sometimes tinged with bronze; undersides are paler and downy.

FRUIT: Smooth, glossy, bright red berries grow profusely in clusters from the leaf axils of female plants. Berry stemlets are short and reddish. The berries are inedible, and may cause intestinal problems.

SEASON: Berries ripen in late summer to early fall. Leaves wither and fall off after a hard frost, but the berries usually persist through midwinter, making a striking display.

COMPARE: Catberry (*I. mucronata*) is related, and similar in growth habit and appearance; however, it is a shorter shrub, usually 10 feet or less in height. Leaf margins are smooth, not toothy; leaves are widest towards the tip and each leaf typically has a short bristle at the tip. Berry stemlets are much longer than those of winterberry. Catberry is found only in the northeastern quarter of the U.S.; in our area, it is most common in northern Wisconsin and Michigan, particularly in the Upper Peninsula.

NOTES: Leaves of winterberry are sometimes dried and used to brew tea. Stems, leafless but with the red berries, are often cut in late fall and used in floral arrangements.

green = key identification feature

LARGE
WOODY SHRUB

ALTERNATE
LEAVES

LATE SUMMER
TO EARLY FALL

Autumn Olive

Elaeagnus umbellata

HABITAT: Open woodlands, grassy areas, waste ground, roadsides and fencerows. Grows in a variety of soils, from sandy, loamy soil to fairly heavy clay soil with good drainage. The roots fix nitrogen, allowing the plant to thrive in poor soils. Does best in full sun, but tolerates light shade.

GROWTH: A large non-native shrub, up to 15 feet tall with equal width. Somewhat straggly, often considered weedy-looking; tends to form thickets. The entire plant has a silvery appearance. Stems are silver-brown, with brown scales. Branches may have scattered small thorns.

LEAVES: Silvery-green leaves grow alternately on short, scaly petioles (stemlets). Leaves are elliptic, 2 to 4 inches long and one-half as wide, tapering at both ends. Undersides are silvery and often have brown dots, especially early in the season. Edges are wavy but untoothed.

FRUIT: Oval to round drupes, ⅓ inch long, are covered with silver scales; fruits are red when ripe. Fruits grow abundantly at leaf axils from short, scaly stemlets. The fruit is delicious, and can be pulped to make fruit leather, jam, sauce or purée; it can also be juiced to use as a beverage or to make jelly. There are no toxic look-alikes.

SEASON: Fruits are hard, brownish and scaly in early summer; as the season progresses, they turn yellow with brown dots, finally ripening to a juicy red at the end of summer or in early fall.

COMPARE: Russet buffaloberry (pg. 134) has similar scales on the fruit, twigs and leaves, but its leaves are opposite and only 1 to 2 inches long. Russian olive (pg. 60) has a similar silvery appearance, but its leaves are much narrower, roughly one-quarter as wide as they are long; ripe fruits are oblong, yellowish and dry with abundant scales. Russian olive is typically thornier than autumn olive.

NOTES: Autumn olive was widely planted during the 1800s in disturbed areas; it is good for stabilizing embankments. It also offers cover and food for wildlife. Nonetheless, it is considered invasive in some areas because it shades out native understory plants and spreads rapidly.

green = key identification feature

Underside of leaf

EDIBLE

LARGE
WOODY SHRUB

ALTERNATE
LEAVES

LATE SUMMER
TO EARLY FALL

Northern Spicebush

Lindera benzoin

HABITAT: Rich, moist deciduous woodlands and streambanks. Also found in ravines, valleys and bottomlands. Prefers full sun to partial shade.

GROWTH: A rounded, open native shrub, 8 to 12 feet in height, with equal spread. All parts of the plant have a **spicy scent**, especially when bruised. The bark is dark brown, and has numerous **small raised, light-colored bumps** scattered along the main stem and older twigs. Spicebush plants are unisexual—a plant is either male or female, and each produces a different type of flower.

LEAVES: Smooth, glossy leaves are oval, tapering on both ends; 2 to 5 inches long, roughly one-half as wide, widest at the midpoint or slightly towards the tip. Edges are smooth; the tip has a sharp point. Leaves are medium green above, lighter below, and grow alternately on the stems on a short petiole (stemlet); veins are prominent on both surfaces. The alternating stems often have several leaves, of widely varying sizes, clustered together.

FRUIT: Shiny oval drupes, about ½ inch long, grow on short stemlets in small clusters along the branches of the female plants; fruits are red when ripe. The base has a small indentation. The fruit is used as a seasoning; it has a spicy, fruity flavor similar to allspice. There are no toxic look-alikes that have the spicy scent of spicebush.

SEASON: Fruits are present on the plant starting in midsummer. They are greenish when immature, ripening in late summer to early fall.

COMPARE: Japanese barberry (pg. 128) has shiny, bright-red, oval-shaped fruits, but barberry shrubs are typically only **3 to 6 feet** tall. Barberry fruits and leaves are also **much smaller** and the plants are **very thorny**.

NOTES: The leaves and twigs can be used to brew a spicy tea. Whitetail deer browse on the plants, as do other woodland mammals, including cottontails and opossums. Songbirds, and upland birds such as quail and pheasants, feed on the fruits. The plant is host to the larval stage of the spicebush swallowtail butterfly.

green = key identification feature

LARGE
WOODY SHRUB

OPPOSITE
LEAVES

LATE SUMMER
TO EARLY FALL

Winged Euonymus

Euonymus alatus

HABITAT: This fast-growing Asian native has been widely planted as an ornamental, and has escaped cultivation to become a nuisance in the wild. It is found in moist, well-drained areas including forest edges, shelterbelts, highway embankments, woodlands and old fields.

GROWTH: A multi-branched shrub up to 20 feet in height; it spreads by suckering and is sometimes seen in wide, tangled masses that can be 50 feet or more in width. Young twigs are green, turning gray and bumpy; as the branches mature, they develop two to four flat, wing-like bark extensions along the branches.

LEAVES: Oval leaves, 1 to 3 inches long with a tapered base and a pointed tip grow oppositely on very short petioles (stemlets). Leaf edges are finely toothed; summer leaves are dull green on top, paler underneath. In fall, leaves gradually turn a vivid magenta-pink; it's common to see a leaf that is part green and part pink.

FRUIT: Egg-shaped, dull pink capsules, about ½ inch long, grow on long stemlets from the leaf axils. Mature capsules split open to reveal seeds with a shiny, bright orangish-red coating. The fruits are inedible.

SEASON: Inconspicuous greenish flowers first appear in spring, and may be present through late summer. The pink capsules develop in late summer, splitting open in early fall.

COMPARE: Wahoo or burning bush (*E. atropurpureus*) is a native plant with similar leaves, growth form and fall color. However, the fruits are four-lobed capsules that don't resemble berries; the stems lack the wing-like extensions. In our area, wahoo is found primarily in the southeast corner of Minnesota and the southern third of Wisconsin.

NOTES: When winged euonymus is in its fall color, it is a stunning plant; it's easy to see why it is frequently used as a landscape specimen. Unfortunately, its aggressive growth habits crowd out native plants, and it is considered an invasive pest. Birds eat the seeds, helping to propagate the plant.

green = key identification feature

Winged bark

TREE

ALTERNATE
LEAVES

SUMMER

*see below

Mulberries

Morus spp.

HABITAT: Two mulberries inhabit our area: the introduced white mulberry (*Morus alba*), and the less-common native red mulberry (*M. rubra*). Both are found in woodlands, fields, urban areas, and along fencelines and road ditches. White mulberry prefers sun, while red mulberry prefers shade and is found in deeper forests.

GROWTH: Medium to large trees; white mulberry is generally 25 to 40 feet high, while red mulberry can grow to 60 feet. Bark of older trees is brown and ridged; white mulberry bark has orange-colored areas between the ridges, while red mulberry bark is uniform in color. White mulberry stems are pinkish-brown; red mulberry's are light tan.

LEAVES: Alternate, with highly variable shape; some have irregular lobes, appearing mitten-like. White mulberry leaves are usually bright green and glossy; they are 3 to 4 inches long with rounded teeth on the edges. Red mulberry leaves are usually deep green and dull with hairy undersides; they are up to 10 inches long with fine, pointed teeth on the edges.

FRUIT: A multiple fruit up to 1 inch long, composed of numerous drupes originating from a cluster of flowers. A short, soft stemlet remains attached to the picked fruit. Ripe white mulberries are red, maroon, deep purple or purplish-black; red mulberries are blackish when ripe. Mulberries are sweet, and can be eaten raw or cooked. There are no toxic look-alikes; however, the fruit must be fully ripe and soft before eating, as unripe fruit and all other parts of the plant are mildly toxic.

SEASON: Fruits ripen in early to mid summer.

COMPARE: No tree resembles mulberries that are bearing fruit.

NOTES: Much confusing information exists about the differences between white and red mulberries. The information presented here relies on an excellent paper, *Red and White Mulberry in Indiana* (Sally S. Weeks; Purdue University). It's easy to identify a mulberry, but hard to determine exact species; however, the differences between them are less important to the forager than to the botanist.

green = key identification feature   * combined range

White mulberry tree and fruit

White mulberry bark

TREE

ALTERNATE
LEAVES

MID TO
LATE SUMMER

American Wild Plum
Prunus americana

HABITAT: Mixed-wood and hardwood forests, particularly along the edges; pastures, thickets on the edges of cultivated areas, streamsides and hedgerows. Does best in full sun; will tolerate some shade, but trees in shade will produce less fruit.

GROWTH: A densely branching native tree or large shrub with a broad crown, up to 25 feet in height with equal spread but often much shorter. The main branches are stiff and dark reddish-brown, with numerous lenticels (breathing pores); side branches are armed with thorns. Older bark is reddish-gray, with a rough texture; it often comes off the tree in large plates. Plum trees may form a thicket.

LEAVES: Oval leaves that taper at both ends are 3 to 4 inches long and roughly one-third as wide; they grow alternately on fairly long petioles (stemlets). Edges are finely toothed; the tip is sharply pointed. Leaves are smooth and deep green above, paler below.

FRUIT: A fleshy, egg-shaped to round drupe with an oval pit, usually about 1 inch across. Fruits have a dusty bloom on the surface, and many have a slight vertical cleft. Ripe fruits are bright reddish-orange, with juicy, sweet, yellowish flesh. Fruits are edible raw or cooked; tastiness varies from plant to plant. There are no toxic look-alikes.

SEASON: Fruits ripen from mid through late summer.

COMPARE: Canadian plum (*P. nigra*), scattered throughout our area, has broader leaves, with blunt, gland-tipped teeth; ripe fruit is yellowish-orange to red, and the trees are more shade-tolerant, often growing in the middle of a forest. Allegheny plum (*P. alleghaniensis*) is found in our area only in parts of Michigan, particularly in the north; its ripe fruit is bluish-purple, and it often grows in a thicket with many dead branches.

NOTES: Plum leaves, stems and pits contain hydrocyanic acid, a cyanide-producing compound. The leaves and pits should never be eaten, and care should be taken to avoid crushing plum pits when juicing the fruits. Cooking or drying eliminates the harmful compound.

green = key identification feature

Thorns on trunk

TREE

ALTERNATE
LEAVES

LATE
SUMMER

Pin Cherry –OR– **Fire Cherry**   *Prunus pensylvanica*

HABITAT: Clearings and edges in mixed-wood forests; hillsides; well-drained riverbanks; rock outcroppings. Prefers sunny sites. Pin cherry is one of the first plants to grow after a forest fire, giving rise to one of its common names, fire cherry.

GROWTH: A small native tree, sometimes appearing like a tall shrub; 3 to 25 feet in height, with an open form and a straight trunk. Bark is reddish-brown and smooth, with prominent raised lenticels (breathing pores); bark on older branches often peels off in horizontal strips.

LEAVES: Narrow, sharp-tipped leaves grow alternately from the stems on reddish petioles (stemlets); leaf edges have fine, rounded teeth and are hairless. Leaves are 3 to 5 inches long, and roughly one-third as wide.

FRUIT: Round, shiny, bright red drupes, about ¼ inch across, grow from reddish stemlets in bunches along the stem. Fruits are translucent when ripe; the large pit can be seen as a shadow in the center of the fruit when the cherries are sunlit. Pin cherries are edible; they're sour when raw but make delicious jelly. There are no toxic look-alikes.

SEASON: Fruits ripen in late summer; the foraging season is usually short because birds relish the cherries and can pick a tree clean very quickly.

COMPARE: Black cherry (pg. 248) has similar narrow, toothy leaves, but fruits are blackish when ripe; the midrib of the leaf has reddish hairs near the base on the lower side. Common chokecherries (pg. 136) have reddish fruits, but leaves are much wider; the fruits grow in long clusters. Sweet cherries (*P. avium*) have wide, oval leaves and fleshy fruits up to 1 inch across; this non-native tree sometimes escapes cultivation and is found scattered in parts of Wisconsin and Michigan.

NOTES: Cherry leaves and pits contain hydrocyanic acid, a cyanide-producing compound. The leaves and pits should never be eaten, and care should be taken to avoid crushing cherry pits when juicing the fruits. Cooking or drying eliminates the harmful compound. Pin cherries have a large pit and thin flesh, so pitting them for a pie would be a thankless task.

green = key identification feature

TREE

OPPOSITE
LEAVES

LATE
SUMMER

Flowering Dogwood

Cornus florida

HABITAT: This native tree is found in areas with cool, moist, well-drained soil; it is common in the understory of hardwood and mixed-wood forests. It prefers ample sunlight, although it will grow in partial shade.

GROWTH: A small tree, typically 25 feet in height or less, with equal or greater width. The tree produces branches fairly close to the ground; they continue up the trunk in a layered fashion. Twigs are green to purplish, and finely hairy; the trunk has dark brownish-gray bark that is broken into square patches. Masses of flowers with four large, white, petal-like bracts appear in spring, before the tree has leafed out.

LEAVES: Oval leaves, 3 to 5 inches long and one-half as wide, grow oppositely on short, grooved petioles (stemlets); the base is tapered and the tip is sharply pointed. Leaves are smooth-edged, or may have very fine teeth (visible with a lens); edges are often slightly wavy. The veins are prominent, curving to follow the leaf edge. Leaves are dark green most of the summer, developing maroon blotches in late summer and turning mottled red in early fall. When a leaf is pulled apart, fine white threads remain between the leaf pieces.

FRUIT: Tight clusters of shiny, bright-red, football-shaped drupes grow at the branch tips; each is ⅓ to ½ inch long and one-third as wide. A black floral remnant is present at the tip. The fruit is very bitter when raw; although it is not toxic, most references consider it inedible.

SEASON: Fruits are green in early summer, ripening to red in late summer; they may persist through winter if not eaten by birds.

COMPARE: Leaves of flowering dogwood resemble other members of the *Cornus* family, but with its distinctive flowers, bright-red fruits, blocky bark and lovely fall color, flowering dogwood is easy to recognize.

NOTES: The fruits are an important winter food source for birds including quail, waxwings, wild turkeys, robins and cardinals; deer browse on the leaves and twigs.

green = key identification feature

TREE

ALTERNATE
LEAVES

SUMMER TO
EARLY FALL

*see below

Hawthorns

Crataegus spp.

HABITAT: Over three dozen species of hawthorns are found in the wild in our area; some are native, while others have escaped cultivation. They hybridize frequently, and identification of exact species in the wild is a matter for specialists. Hawthorns inhabit rocky areas, pastures, old fields and woodlots, sun-dappled mixed-wood forests, and shelterbelts. Trees in sunny areas produce the most fruit.

GROWTH: Small to medium trees, occasionally appearing as large shrubs; height varies from 6 feet to over 40 feet. Hawthorns often have a rounded crown and widely spreading branches. Thorns—often long and sharp, as in the photo at right—are always present on wild hawthorns, but may be negligible or absent on cultivated varieties which have escaped into the wild. Bark on the main trunk is usually dark gray and roughly textured, with vertical fissures; young stems are smooth and gray-brown.

LEAVES: Hawthorn leaves are sharply toothed, although specific shape is variable. The most easily identifiable hawthorns have leaves that are broadly tapered and smooth-edged at the base, with coarse, sharp teeth from the end of the base to the tip. Some species have toothy lobes; others are oval, like crabapple leaves but with larger, sharper teeth. Leaves are typically 2 to 4 inches long, and grow alternately.

FRUIT: Pomes, generally oval with slightly flattened sides; they have a crown on the bottom and grow on a long stemlet. Fruits are generally reddish when ripe, but may be yellowish; size ranges from ¼ to 1 inch across. All hawthorns are edible; there are no toxic look-alikes.

SEASON: Hawthorns ripen from midsummer to early fall.

COMPARE: Crabapples (pg. 162) are similar, but leaves are more reliably oval-shaped, with finer, rounded teeth; their fruit is generally rounder.

NOTES: Before harvesting hawthorns, taste a few from the tree you're considering. The best hawthorns have a fair amount of juicy flesh in proportion to the seeds; flesh may be soft and tender, or crunchy like an apple, and the flavor is often reminiscent of pears.

green = key identification feature

* combined range

TREE

ALTERNATE
LEAVES

LATE SUMMER
TO FALL

*see below

Crabapples –AND– Apples

Malus spp.

HABITAT: Numerous crabapple varieties grow in the wild throughout our area; they tend to hybridize, and exact identification is difficult. Crabapples (various *Malus* spp.) are found in a variety of habitats, including open woods, thickets, old fields, streambanks, parks and grasslands. Apples (*M. pumila*), originally from Asia, grow in abandoned orchards and on old homestead sites; they are also found where apple cores have been discarded by hikers and in areas where people feed them to wildlife.

GROWTH: Both are small to medium trees, with a rounded crown and many branches; they may be as short as 5 feet, or as tall as 30 feet, generally with equal or greater spread. Young stems are dark reddish-brown, with numerous pale lenticels (breathing pores); older stems are gray and coarsely textured. Native crabapples have thorns; some domestic escapees are thornless. Apple trees are thornless.

LEAVES: Oval leaves, tapered at both ends, grow alternately on long petioles (stemlets), often in small clusters that alternate along the branch; Toringo or Siebold crab (*M. toringo*) also has some lobed leaves. Leaves are 1 to 5 inches long, and generally one-third as wide; margins are toothy, but the teeth may be rounded or sharp depending on the species.

FRUIT: Both are rounded pomes. Crabapples often have a crown on the base; some, such as Toringo crabs, have an indented spot instead. Crabapples grow on a long, thin stemlet; apple stemlets are stubby. Depending on species, crabapples may be yellow, pink or red, and ½ to 1½ inches across. Apples are red, or yellow with an overall red blush; the skin is dotted with pale speckles, and often has coarse brown or yellowish blotches. All crabapples and apples are edible; some are bitter. There are no toxic look-alikes.

SEASON: Both ripen in late summer to fall; crabapples may also ripen earlier.

COMPARE: Hawthorns (pg. 160) have similar fruit, but leaves are coarsely toothed and trees are thornier; fruits are generally oval.

NOTES: Eating quality of crabapples and apples varies from tree to tree, and also between species. Sample a few before harvesting.

green = key identification feature   * combined range; specific locations not available

Crabapple

Toringo crab

Apple

TREE   ALTERNATE   LATE SUMMER
        COMPOUND   THROUGH FALL
        LEAVES   *see below

Smooth Sumac
–AND– Staghorn Sumac

Rhus glabra, R. typhina

HABITAT: These native trees grow in sunny fields and w, disturbed areas, road ditches and embankments, waste ground.

GROWTH: Small trees up to 15 feet tall, sometimes appearing as large shrubs. Sumac spreads via rhizomes (underground root-bearing stems), and usually grows in dense colonies. Smooth sumac (*Rhus glabra*) has smooth twigs and leafstalks; those of staghorn sumac (*R. typhina*) are covered with fine, dense hairs. Bark of both is dark and smooth.

LEAVES: Pinnately (feather-like) compound leaves, each with 11 to 31 leaflets, grow alternately. Leaves are 12 to 24 inches long. Leaflets are 2 to 5 inches long, lance-shaped with toothy edges; deep green on top, paler underneath. Leafstalks of smooth sumac are reddish; those of staghorn sumac are greenish to tan.

FRUIT: Large, cone-shaped clusters of fuzzy, deep-red drupes grow upright at the end of the branches, rising above the leaves. Smooth sumac has clusters that are irregular; often, two or three clusters of various sizes grow side-by-side at the end of the branch. Staghorn sumac has a single, fairly symmetrical cluster at the end of the branch. Clusters are typically 3 to 6 inches long. The drupes are lemony-sour, and can be used to make a lemonade-type beverage. There are no toxic look-alikes with deep-red fruits; however, people who are highly allergic to poison ivy, mangoes or cashews should avoid all sumacs, which are in the same family and may cause a severe allergic reaction.

SEASON: Sumac clusters ripen in late summer, and persist on the plant through winter, although their flavor is washed away by fall rains.

COMPARE: Winged sumac (pg. 180) is similar in overall appearance, but the leafstalk has green wing-like extensions between the leaflets; its fruit clusters are purplish in the summer, ripening to red in the fall.

NOTES: Strain sumac lemonade to remove tiny hairs that irritate the throat.

green = key identification feature   * combined range

Smooth sumac

Staghorn sumac

TENDER
LEAFY PLANT

WHORLED
LEAVES

MID TO
LATE SUMMER
*see below

Indian Cucumber

Medeola virginiana

HABITAT: This native perennial inhabits open, well-drained areas in moist, mixed-wood, coniferous or deciduous forests; also found along the edges of bogs and swamps.

GROWTH: A single stem, up to 2½ feet in height, grows from a rhizome (underground root-bearing stem). Most plants have **two whorls of leaves**: a larger whorl about midway up the stem, and a smaller whorl, with fewer leaves, at the top. Smaller plants have only the larger whorl; it sits on top of the stem, which is shorter than a stem on a plant with two whorls. Berries are produced on plants with two whorls.

LEAVES: The large whorl consists of five to nine lance-shaped leaves radiating from the stem. These leaves are 2½ to 4½ inches long and one-third to one-half as wide, tapering to points on both ends. The smaller whorl consists of three to five leaves that are lance-shaped but broader than those of the lower whorl; these leaves are 1¼ to 2¼ inches long and have more rounded bases. All leaves have parallel veins; they are smooth and shiny, with smooth edges.

FRUIT: Round, glossy, dark purple berries, each ⅛ to ⅓ inch across, **grow on short, erect stemlets** in a cluster from the **center of the upper whorl**; stemlets are red when the berries are ripe. The berries are inedible.

SEASON: Yellow flowers bloom in early summer; berries follow and are ripe from mid to late summer. The leaves usually have withered by the time the berries are ripe.

COMPARE: Several plants in our area have similar whorled leaves, but their fruits are different. Black snakeroot (*Sanicula marilandica*; found throughout our area) has whorled leaves that grow in two tiers, but it produces a **pod**, not berries. Starflower (*Trientalis borealis*; found throughout most of our area except southeastern Minnesota) also has whorled leaves, but it is much shorter, with just a **single whorl**; its fruit is a **dry capsule**.

NOTES: The rhizome of Indian cucumber can be eaten; it has a cucumber-like taste.

green = key identification feature   * specific MN locations not available

Unripe berries

Ripe berries

TENDER
LEAFY PLANT

ALTERNATE
COMPOUND
LEAVES

LATE SUMMER
TO FALL

American Spikenard

Aralia racemosa

HABITAT: This native plant is found in rich, open deciduous and mixed-wood forests, thickets, wooded slopes and ravines. It prefers moist, well-drained soil, and grows in full sun to part shade.

GROWTH: A very large, bushy, somewhat top-heavy plant that is almost shrub-like and grows from an underground rhizome (root-bearing stem). Typically 3 to 5 feet in height, with equal width near the top; white flowers grow in numerous long, loose, upright clusters that have an overall conical shape. Stems are soft and greenish-purple, with fine hairs.

LEAVES: Large doubly-compound leaves, each with three divisions, grow alternately on the stems; overall leaf length is up to 3 feet. Each of the three divisions has three to five heart-shaped leaflets that are 3 to 6 inches in length and two-thirds as wide, with doubly-toothed edges and a pointed tip. Leaflets are green and slightly hairy on both surfaces; leaflet nodes are often purplish.

FRUIT: Round drupes, each up to ¼ inch across, replace the flowers in the long, loose clusters (racemes); drupes are greenish when young, ripening to reddish-purple. The effect is that of a long column of tiny grapes. The fruits have a sharp aftertaste; some sources list them as edible, while others say they should not be eaten.

SEASON: Spikenard flowers in mid to late summer; fruits ripen from late summer to fall.

COMPARE: Bristly sarsaparilla (*A. hispida*; found in roughly the same range but less common) is similar in appearance, but smaller overall, with much smaller leaves; its stems are covered with bristly hairs, and its fruits grow in rounded clusters rather than long racemes. All parts of the plant have an unpleasant odor. Fruits of bristly sarsaparilla are not edible.

NOTES: Like its much smaller relative sarsaparilla (pg. 212), spikenard has aromatic, spicy-flavored rhizomes that are often used as a flavoring agent. The young shoot tips can also be cooked as a vegetable.

green = key identification feature

VINING
PLANT

ALTERNATE
LEAVES

LATE SUMMER
TO EARLY FALL
*see below

Wild Grapes

Vitis spp.

HABITAT: Three native wild grape species grow in our region. Riverbank grapes (*Vitis riparia*) are the most common, and grow throughout the region. Summer grapes (*V. aestivalis*) are found in southern Wisconsin and southern Michigan; fox grapes (*V. labrusca*) are scattered in southern Michigan. All prefer full sun, and inhabit moist, rich areas including tangles, thickets, river and streambanks and woodland margins.

GROWTH: A straggling, woody vine that uses coiling tendrils to anchor itself on other plants, fences, poles or buildings. Riverbank grapes may be 70 feet long; summer grapes and fox grapes are generally 35 feet or less. Young stems of all three are greenish and flexible; older stems are reddish-brown or brownish-gray, and usually have shaggy bark.

LEAVES: Toothy leaves up to 6 inches long grow alternately on long petioles (stemlets). Leaves are heart-shaped, usually with shallow or indistinct lobes; summer and fox grape vines may have a few deeply lobed leaves. Teeth on riverbank leaves are coarse and sharp, while those on summer and fox grapes are finer and often rounded. Leaves of summer and fox grapes are white or whitish-tan on the undersides; those of riverbank grapes are pale green on the undersides.

FRUIT: A tight cluster of edible round, juicy berries hangs from the vine on a sturdy stalk, opposite a leaf. Berries grow on short stemlets; each has one to six small, oval or pear-shaped seeds. Riverbank and summer grapes are ¼ to ½ inch across; fox grapes are up to ¾ inch across. Wild grapes are purplish-blue to purplish-black when ripe, with a whitish bloom.

SEASON: Fruits ripen in late summer to early fall.

COMPARE: Several plants in our area have round, purplish fruits that are inedible or toxic. They are Canada moonseed (pg. 172), five-leaved ivy (pg. 188) and the *Smilax* species (pg. 218). For more detail, please see "Be certain, be safe: Wild grapes" on pgs. 22–23.

NOTES: All wild grapes are edible; fruits from individual plants may be sour or sweet, regardless of variety.

green = key identification feature

* combined range

Riverbank grapes

Fox grapes

Summer grape leaves, immature fruit

VINING
PLANT

ALTERNATE
LEAVES

LATE SUMMER
TO EARLY FALL

Canada Moonseed

Menispermum canadense

HABITAT: Streambanks, thickets, moist woody areas. Prefers full sun.

GROWTH: This native woody vine reaches up to 20 feet in length. Unlike wild grapes (pg. 170), moonseed has no tendrils, and climbs by coiling its central stem around the host. Younger stems are hairy, greenish or reddish and flexible; older stems are smooth, bronze to dark reddish-brown and woody.

LEAVES: Alternate, with three to seven shallow lobes; edges are smooth and untoothed. The long petiole (stemlet) is attached to the underside of the leaf, slightly away from the base (peltate). The upper surface is smooth and light green; the underside is silvery-green with fine hairs. Leaves are 4 to 7 inches long, and equally wide.

FRUIT: Purplish-blue to purplish-black drupes with a whitish bloom, each containing a single flat seed shaped like a broad crescent (a circle with a bite taken away). Drupes are round and ¼ to ⅓ inch across; they grow in loose clusters that hang from the vine on a long, spindly fruit stalk, opposite a leaf. They are highly toxic.

SEASON: Moonseed fruits are ripe in late summer to early fall, at about the same time as wild grapes.

COMPARE: Moonseed bears an unfortunate resemblance to wild grapes (pg. 170). However, the leaves of wild grapes have toothy edges, and are attached directly to the petiole; those of moonseed have smooth edges and peltate attachment. Grapes have one to six small, oval or pear-shaped seeds, rather than the single crescent-shaped seed that gives moonseed its common name. Finally, grapes attach themselves to hosts by using tendrils, which are absent on moonseed. It is very important to pay strict attention when harvesting wild grapes, to avoid gathering any moonseed fruits, which are toxic.

NOTES: Moonseed fruits contain the alkaloid dauricine, a compound that affects the heart. Its use in medicine is being studied, but it is toxic in its natural form as found in moonseed.

green = key identification feature

Fruits and seed

SMALL
WOODY SHRUB

ALTERNATE
LEAVES

MID TO
LATE SUMMER

*see below

Purplish Gooseberries

Ribes spp.

HABITAT: Two native gooseberry shrubs with purplish fruits grow in our area. Prickly or pasture gooseberry (*Ribes cynosbati*) is found in thickets, tangles, moist woods and rocky areas. Swamp or smooth gooseberry (*R. hirtellum*) is found in similar locations, but also grows in boggy areas.

GROWTH: Both are arching shrubs about 3 feet high. Leaf nodes of prickly gooseberry have one to three thorns; smooth gooseberry's thorns may be weak or absent. Prickly gooseberry stems have scattered bristles; mature stems of swamp gooseberry have sparse to no bristles, although young stems have small bristles or hairs.

LEAVES: Attached alternately to the stem by a petiole (stemlet); leaf nodes have up to three leaves. Each leaf has three to five lobes, resembling a rounded maple leaf. Prickly gooseberry leaves have rounded teeth, and the leaf bases are often heart-shaped. Swamp gooseberry leaves have sharper teeth, and the bases are wedge-shaped or flat.

FRUIT: The ¼- to ½-inch round berry grows on a thin stemlet from leaf nodes, singly or in small clusters. Distinct stripes run longitudinally on the berry; a long flower remnant, often called a pigtail, is present at the end of the berry. Prickly gooseberries are reddish-purple when ripe, with soft prickles, either overall or on the half of the fruit closest to the stem. Swamp gooseberries are often darker and lack prickles. Gooseberries are edible in both the green and ripe stages.

SEASON: Ripe fruits are present from mid to late summer.

COMPARE: Fruits of Missouri and northern gooseberries (pg. 226) are smooth, and blackish-purple when ripe; stems of both are generally bristly. Currant shrubs (pgs. 120, 228) resemble gooseberry shrubs, but berries are smaller and grow in long, hanging clusters of multiple fruits.

NOTES: Ripe gooseberries are excellent in baked desserts, sauces and other dishes. Green gooseberries (pg. 46) are used for jam and jelly. You don't have to wait for gooseberries to ripen fully before picking, since they are edible even when green (as long as they are soft).

green = key identification feature

* combined range

Prickly gooseberry

Swamp gooseberry

LARGE
WOODY SHRUB

OPPOSITE
COMPOUND
LEAVES

LATE
SUMMER

Common Elderberry

Sambucus canadensis

HABITAT: This native shrub grows in moist areas, including woodland edges, shelterbelts, thickets, abandoned fields, roadsides, meadows, river and streambanks, and ditch edges. It prefers full sun to part shade.

GROWTH: An open shrub, 5 to 12 feet in height, with a broad, rounded crown. Branches are yellowish-gray, with numerous warty lenticels (breathing pores); older bark is greenish or gray, streaked with white. White flowers grow in large, showy umbrella-like clusters; stemlets are reddish. When the flowers fall and berries are developing, the plant is easy to spot because of the groupings of rounded, purplish flower stemlets, which have a lacy appearance.

LEAVES: Compound leaves, each with 5 to 11 leaflets, grow oppositely on the stem; leaves are 6 to 10 inches long and nearly as wide. Leaflets are 2 to 4 inches long and one-half as wide, broadly oval and tapered on both ends; edges are sharply toothed. The top sides are dark green and smooth; the undersides are paler and may be downy.

FRUIT: Round berries, about ⁳⁄₁₆ inch in diameter with three to five seeds, grow in drooping, flat-topped clusters (cymes). Berries are green when immature, ripening to deep purple or purplish-black; stemlets are reddish-purple. The berries are edible, and are juiced to make jelly, jam and wine. Leaves, stems, seeds and all other parts of all elderberry species are toxic.

SEASON: Flowers appear in early summer; fruits ripen in late summer.

COMPARE: Red elderberry (pg. 132) has similar growth habit and leaves, but its berries are bright red and grow in rounded clusters, rather than the flat-topped clusters of common elderberry. Red elderberry, which is inedible, ripens a month or more before common elderberry.

NOTES: Some sources list this plant as *Sambucus nigra* ssp. *canadensis*. Elderberry flowers are used to make a delicate wine; an infusion of the flowers is also used to treat headache. Flower clusters are sometimes gathered before the flowers open, then battered and deep-fried.

green = key identification feature

LARGE SHRUB
OR SMALL TREE

ALTERNATE
LEAVES

SUMMER

*see below

Serviceberries

Amelanchier spp.

HABITAT: Eight varieties of serviceberry are native to our area; all produce edible fruits with a similar appearance. Found in mixed-wood forests and thickets. They may grow as a single specimen, or in groups. Saskatoon (*Amelanchier alnifolia*), low (*A. humilis*) and running serviceberries (*A. stolonifera*; also listed as *A. spicata*) spread by rhizomes (underground root-bearing stems), and form colonies; running serviceberry often grows in **extremely rocky areas**, sometimes growing from cracks in bedrock.

GROWTH: An erect shrub or small tree, usually 3 to 15 feet tall; Allegheny serviceberry (*A. laevis*) may grow to **40 feet**. Bark is smooth, and usually gray or brownish; older bark may have vertical furrows. Roundleaf serviceberry (*A. sanguinea*) has **reddish-brown twigs and branches**.

LEAVES: Oval to egg-shaped leaves, 1 to 3 inches long, are bright green on top, paler below. The undersides may have small, fine hairs; downy serviceberry (*A. arborea*) and inland serviceberry (*A. interior*) are **densely hairy** underneath. Leaf edges, particularly the top half, are toothy; low, Saskatoon, running and roundleaf serviceberry leaves have fairly coarse teeth, while the others are finely toothed. Leaves of Saskatoon serviceberries often appear nearly **rectangular**.

FRUIT: Pomes with **crowns on the bottom** (similar to blueberries) grow on long stemlets along a separate fruiting stem; fruits have a whitish bloom. Mountain serviceberry (*A. bartramiana*) has three or fewer fruits per cluster, while others have four or more. Most are sweet and delicious, with a pear-like flavor; the tiny, soft seeds are unnoticeable. Ripe fruits range from reddish-purple, to blue, to purple, to black; judge ripeness by texture, choosing soft fruits to harvest. There are no toxic look-alikes.

SEASON: Serviceberry fruits are ripe from early to late summer, depending on the species and location.

COMPARE: Chokecherries (pg. 136) have similar leaves, but the fruits are smaller and **translucent**, with **no crown** on the bottom.

NOTES: Also called Juneberry, a reference to their blooming time.

green = key identification feature   * combined range

LARGE SHRUB
OR SMALL TREE

ALTERNATE
COMPOUND
LEAVES

LATE SUMMER
THROUGH FALL

Winged –OR– **Shining Sumac**

Rhus copallinum

HABITAT: This native plant is found in old fields and disturbed areas, along-side roads, in open woods and sandy areas, and on rocky outcrops. It prefers sun, and can tolerate drought. Some sources list it as *R. copallina*.

GROWTH: A large, open shrub or small tree, ranging from 3 to 20 feet in height. Sumac spreads readily via rhizomes (underground root-bearing stems), and is usually seen in dense colonies. Twigs are reddish-brown to gray, with numerous lenticels (breathing pores); young twigs are downy. Older bark is gray to brown, with a rough texture. Dense clusters of tiny yellowish flowers grow upright from the end of the branch; the flowers are present from late spring through late summer.

LEAVES: Pinnately (feather-like) compound leaves, each with 7 to 15 leaflets (some accounts say up to 23), grow alternately. Leaves are up to 12 inches long. Leaflets are 1 to 3 inches long and lance-shaped; they are glossy and deep green on top, paler and downy underneath. Edges are typically smooth, although some fine teeth may be present. **Leafstalks have flat, wing-like green extensions between the leaflets.** Leaves turn brilliant red in fall.

FRUIT: Cone-shaped clusters of fuzzy, sticky purplish or pink drupes develop at the end of the branches starting in midsummer; fruits turn deep maroon in late summer to fall. Clusters are 3 to 5 inches long and often droop or hang down. The drupes are lemony-sour, and can be used to make a lemonade-type beverage. There are no toxic look-alikes that have purplish, pink or red fruits; however, people who are highly allergic to poison ivy, mangoes, or cashews should avoid all sumacs, which are in the same family and may cause a severe allergic reaction.

SEASON: Sumac clusters ripen in late summer through fall, and persist on the plant through winter; their flavor is washed away by fall rains.

COMPARE: Smooth and staghorn sumac (pg. 164) are similar, but leafstalks lack the wings; fruits are deep red and the fruit clusters stand upright.

NOTES: Strain sumac lemonade to remove tiny hairs that irritate the throat.

green = key identification feature

Fully ripe cluster

TENDER
LEAFY PLANT

BASAL
LEAF GROWTH

SUMMER

Clintonia
–OR– **Blue-Bead Lily**

Clintonia borealis

HABITAT: This native plant inhabits cool, sun-dappled mixed-wood and coniferous forests. It is common in the boreal forest.

GROWTH: Bright-green, glossy leaves grow basally from the underground rhizome (root-bearing stem). Flowers, followed by fruit, are borne on a separate, leafless stalk which rises above the leaves from the center of the plant. Clintonia is generally about a foot high.

LEAVES: Smooth, glossy paddle-shaped leaves are up to 10 inches long and one-third as wide; the base is tapered and the tip is broad, ending in a small point. Leaves are deeply cleft by the midrib; edges are smooth, with tiny hairs (visible with a lens). Each plant typically has three leaves, but may have up to five or only two.

FRUIT: Glossy, opaque berries with a deep dimple at the end grow in a small cluster on the flower stalk. The berry is a slightly flattened oval, up to ⅓ inch across; it is white when unripe, turning bright or deep metallic blue. Fruits are mildly toxic and should not be eaten.

SEASON: Nodding, bell-shaped yellow flowers appear in early summer; the berries follow, ripening by midsummer.

COMPARE: Lowbush blueberries (pg. 190) have blue berries, but they have a dusty white bloom and a crown on the bottom; the plants are low-growing woody shrubs. Although clintonia plants don't resemble blueberries at all, care should be taken when in the woods with children, who may mistake the highly visible blue berries of clintonia as the edible blueberry.

NOTES: Leaves from young clintonia, picked just as the plants start to flower, are edible, with a delightful, fresh, cucumber-like taste. By the time the plants have berries, the leaves are tough and bitter, and are no longer considered edible.

green = key identification feature

TENDER
LEAFY PLANT

ALTERNATE
LEAVES

MID TO
LATE SUMMER

Smooth Solomon's Seal

Polygonatum biflorum

HABITAT: This native plant is found in rich, moist mixed-wood and deciduous forests, waste ground, urban areas, roadside ditches and thickets; it also grows along the edges of streams and ponds.

GROWTH: A single stem grows in a long arch from the underground rhizome (root-bearing stem). Smooth Solomon's seal is the largest of the Solomon's seal family, and is often called great Solomon's seal because of its size. The stem can grow up to 5 feet in length, although it is usually much shorter; longer stems arch gracefully, making the plant appear shorter than it is.

LEAVES: Lance-shaped leaves with many parallel veins grow alternately, attached directly to the stem or slightly clasping; leaves are 2 to 7 inches in length and are typically narrow. Topsides are green and smooth; undersides are paler, with hairless veins. Leaves are broadest near the base, tapering to a point; edges are smooth and hairless.

FRUIT: Round, dark blue berries, about ⅓ inch across with a slight vertical cleft, grow in small groups or singly from the leaf axils. Berries have a slight bloom, and grow from thin stemlets. They are inedible.

SEASON: Berries mature in mid to late summer.

COMPARE: The only other "true" Solomon's seal that grows in our area is hairy Solomon's seal (*P. pubescens*). Like smooth Solomon's seal, berries of hairy Solomon's seal grow from the leaf axils; however, the plant is shorter, generally 3 feet or less in length, and leaves grow on short petioles (stemlets); edges of the leaf, and leaf veins on the undersides, have fine hairs, and there are only one to four berries at each leaf axil. All other Solomon's seals in our area are "false," having the berries growing from the tip of the stem. Please see the false Solomon's seal text on pg. 36 for more information about plants with similar appearance.

NOTES: The rhizome of smooth Solomon's seal is edible when cooked; however, the plant is protected in much of its range and should be harvested only where abundant (and legal).

green = key identification feature

Overview of plant

TENDER
LEAFY PLANT

COMPOUND
LEAVES

LATE
SUMMER

Blue Cohosh

Caulophyllum thalictroides

HABITAT: Rich, moist mixed-wood and deciduous forests, valleys, river bottoms and floodplains. Grows best in shade or dappled sun.

GROWTH: A leafy, native plant that grows from an underground rhizome (root-bearing stem). The main stem divides into two stems, each with compound leaves that are sub-divided into three stalks. Stalks on the lower leaf each have three to nine leaflets. The upper leaf is smaller; each stalk typically has three leaflets. A separate, leafless flowering stalk rises above the leaves. Blue cohosh is typically 12 to 18 inches in height, but it can reach 3 feet. It often forms colonies.

LEAVES: Blue cohosh has many leaves, growing in a complex pattern as described above. Leaves are up to 12 inches long; individual leaflets are 1 to 3 inches long and often as wide. Leaflets are typically tulip-shaped and have rounded lobes ending in a shallow point, generally three lobes per leaflet but sometimes two.

FRUIT: What appears to be a berry is actually the seed of the plant; it is round and covered by a thinly fleshy, deep-blue coat with a powdery bloom. Each is about ⅜ inch across; the stemlet is thin and green where it joins the flowering stalk, thickening where it joins the seed to somewhat resemble a tiny blue light bulb. The fruits are inedible.

SEASON: Seeds have a greenish coat in early summer; the coat turns blue by late summer.

COMPARE: Giant blue cohosh (*C. giganteum*; in our area, found scattered in Michigan) is similar but slightly larger, with fewer fruits. Lowbush blueberries (pg. 190) have blue berries, but they have a crown on the bottom. Although blue cohosh plants don't resemble blueberries, care should be taken when in the woods with children, who may mistake the highly visible blue berries of blue cohosh as the edible blueberry.

NOTES: Blue cohosh root has been used to induce labor, and to treat other gynecological conditions. Raw seeds are regarded as toxic, but some sources report that they can be roasted and used as a coffee substitute.

green = key identification feature

VINING
PLANT

ALTERNATE
COMPOUND
LEAVES

LATE SUMMER
TO EARLY FALL

*see below

Five-Leaved Ivy

Parthenocissus spp.

HABITAT: Moist, well-drained areas, including forest edges, cliff bases, streambanks, fencerows, ravines and urban areas. Prefers sun.

GROWTH: Two native *Parthenocissus* species share so many of the same characteristics that it is difficult to separate them. These include Virginia creeper (*P. quinquefolia*) and woodbine (*P. vitacea*, also listed as *P. inserta*). Both are sprawling, native vines that uses tendrils to climb or otherwise attach themselves to other plants and supporting structures; individual stems may be 70 feet or longer. Young stems are green to tan; older stems are brownish and woody, with rough, shreddy bark. The easiest difference to spot between the two plants is that Virginia creeper's tendrils have many branches, which have sucker feet that the plant uses for attachment. Virginia creeper develops aerial roots where it is in contact with a tree. Woodbine tendrils have only two or three branches and lack the sucker feet; the plant uses its tendrils to coil around objects.

LEAVES: Palmately compound leaves typically have five leaflets; they average 7 inches across and grow alternately on long petioles (stemlets). Leaflets are oval with tapering ends and a pointed tip; edges have sharp teeth. The two leaflets at the base are smaller than the others. Leaf undersides are paler than the top side. Leaves turn bright scarlet in early fall.

FRUIT: Round berries, about ⅓ inch across, grow in loose, open clusters on bright pink stemlets originating opposite a leaf. Ripe berries are deep bluish-purple with a dusty bloom. Many sources list the berries as toxic; others say they are edible but not tasty. They contain calcium oxalate, which may irritate the throat. It's best to avoid them.

SEASON: Berries ripen in late summer to early fall, and may persist on the plant after the leaves drop in the fall.

COMPARE: Berries resemble wild grapes (pg. 170), but grapes grow in tighter clusters and the berry stemlets are tan or greenish. When picking grapes, do not pick any fruits growing on hot-pink berry stemlets.

NOTES: The berries of five-leaved ivy are eaten by many species of birds.

green = key identification feature

* combined range

Fall leaf color

SMALL
WOODY SHRUB

ALTERNATE
LEAVES

MID TO
LATE SUMMER

*see below

Low-Growing Blueberries

Vaccinium spp.

HABITAT: Rocky or gravelly areas on the edges of coniferous and mixed-wood forests; clearings; along footpaths; sunny hilltops and ridges. Blueberries are one of the first plants to appear after a forest fire.

GROWTH: Three types of native, low-growing blueberries are found in our area: lowbush blueberry (*Vaccinium angustifolium*), velvet-leaf blueberry (*V. myrtilloides*) and hillside blueberries (*V. pallidum*; also called Blue Ridge blueberry). All are low, sprawling, woody shrubs, up to 3 feet in height; they often grow in spreading colonies.

LEAVES: The oval leaves taper on both ends, coming to a softly pointed tip. Lowbush blueberry leaves are up to 1½ inches long; those of velvet-leaf and hillside blueberries are up to 2 inches long. Leaves are deep green to bluish-green and sometimes tinged with red; those of lowbush and hillside blueberries are smooth, while velvet-leaf blueberry leaves are softly hairy. Leaves of all species attach alternately to the stems on short petioles (stemlets).

FRUIT: Round berries have a prominent five-pointed crown on the bottom; when ripe, they are blue with a dusty bloom. Berries are ¼ to ⅓ inch across, and have paler flesh with small, soft seeds that are unnoticeable. They grow in tight clusters at the ends of twigs or short stemlets. Ripe blueberries are delicious raw or cooked. Although there are other plants with berries that are blue, there are no toxic look-alikes as long as good identification practices are followed.

SEASON: Berries ripen in mid to late summer.

COMPARE: Bilberries (pg. 192) resemble blueberries, but fruits grow singly or in pairs. Black huckleberries (pg. 230) look similar, but ripe fruits are blackish; leaves have yellow resin dots on the underside. Highbush blueberries (pg. 202) have similar fruits, but they grow as woody shrubs up to 10 feet in height. Fruits of all three are edible and delicious.

NOTES: Blueberries are one of the most popular wild fruits in our region; they are a breakfast favorite at many campsites.

green = key identification feature

* combined range

Lowbush blueberries

SMALL
WOODY SHRUB

ALTERNATE
LEAVES

MID TO
LATE SUMMER

Dwarf Bilberry

Vaccinium cespitosum

HABITAT: Open areas in coniferous forests; dry, sandy areas; sometimes found seasonally in meadow-like areas. It is uncommon in our area, appearing more frequently in Canada and in the western states, and is listed as threatened in Michigan.

GROWTH: This native plant is a low-growing, dense shrub, up to 1 foot in height but generally shorter; it often spreads in circular, mat-like colonies. Stems are greenish to reddish, and may be smooth or have sparse, tiny hairs (visible with a lens).

LEAVES: Paddle-shaped, widest above the midpoint with a tapering base. Tips may be blunt or roundly pointed. The upper half of the leaf has fine, bristle-tipped teeth. Leaves are bright green, sometimes tinged with red, and shiny on both sides; they are typically ½ to 1 inch long and one-third as wide, and grow alternately on the stems.

FRUIT: Round berries have a subtle five-pointed crown on the bottom; when ripe, they are bluish-purple to deep violet with a dusty bloom. Berries are typically ¼ inch across, and have reddish or purplish flesh. They grow singly or in pairs at the end of short stemlets originating in the leaf axils. Ripe bilberries are delicious raw or cooked. Although there are other plants with berries that are blue, there are no toxic look-alikes as long as good identification practices are followed.

SEASON: Bilberries ripen in mid to late summer.

COMPARE: Blueberries (pg. 190, 202) are similar, but the berries grow in tight clusters and the crown is more prominent; flesh of blueberries is greenish, while that of bilberries is reddish. Huckleberries (pg. 230) also look similar, but ripe fruits are blackish. Oval-leaf bilberry (*V. ovalifolium*), found in our area only in Michigan's Upper Peninsula, has oval leaves with smooth edges; its blue fruits grow singly from the leaf axils. All three plants have oval rather than paddle-shaped leaves, and are taller.

NOTES: Dwarf bilberry is the host plant for the northern blue butterfly. This plant is also listed as *V. caespitosum*.

green = key identification feature

SMALL
WOODY SHRUB

OPPOSITE
LEAVES

MID TO
LATE SUMMER

Mountain Fly Honeysuckle

Lonicera villosa

HABITAT: This native plant inhabits moist areas including streambanks, swamp edges, peat bogs and lakeshores. Also found in rocky areas with good moisture, and in damp, sun-dappled mixed-wood or coniferous forests. Prefers full or part sun; will not produce fruit in shady areas.

GROWTH: A small, open shrub, generally 3 feet high or less. Branches are greenish to purplish and finely hairy when young, turning reddish-brown to gray and developing shreddy bark with age.

LEAVES: Opposite, with short petioles (stemlets); up to 2½ inches in length and less than one-half as wide. Leaves taper on both ends and are widest above the midpoint; tips are rounded or softly pointed. Top and bottom surfaces are hairy; edges are fringed with hairs. Leaves are medium green above and lighter beneath, and grow close together, giving a crowded, bunched appearance.

FRUIT: Slightly oblong berries, about ½ inch long, grow in pairs from the leaf axil on the end of a short stalk. Ripe berries are deep blue, and have a whitish bloom. The berries are edible and have a slightly bitter undertone. Although there are other plants with berries that are blue, there are no toxic look-alikes as long as good identification practices are followed.

SEASON: Light yellow flowers appear in early summer; fruits ripen in mid to late summer.

COMPARE: Swamp fly honeysuckle (pg. 122) grows in the same areas and looks similar to mountain fly honeysuckle, but it has red berries and smooth, hairless leaves. Blueberries (pgs. 190, 202) have blue fruits that grow in clusters, not paired like those of mountain fly honeysuckle. Bilberries (pg. 192) have bluish-purple fruits that grow singly or in pairs, but the leaves are paddle-shaped, with toothy tips.

NOTES: Mountain fly honeysuckle berries can be eaten raw but are usually used to make jam or baked goods. Mountain fly honeysuckle is a native plant, unlike the bush honeysuckles on pg. 140.

green = key identification feature

SMALL
WOODY SHRUB

ALTERNATE
LEAVES

LATE
SUMMER

Common Juniper

Juniperus communis

HABITAT: Dry, sunny openings in mixed-wood and coniferous forests; also found on rocky outcrops, ridges and exposed slopes.

GROWTH: In our area, common juniper is a **sprawling evergreen shrub**, up to 4 feet in height, with short branches that tend to grow upright. It can also grow as a tree, but that form is not generally found in our area. Bark is reddish-brown, fibrous and shreddy. Common juniper is unisexual—a plant is either male or female, and each produces a different type of fruit.

LEAVES: Narrow, pointed, awl-like evergreen needles, about ½ inch in length, grow alternately in clusters of three; they have a strong smell which is both piney and resinous. Needles are **concave on top, with a whitish center**; undersides are dark green. Except near the tip of the branch, needles usually grow almost perpendicular to the branches, giving each branch a bushy appearance.

FRUIT: The female fruit is a round, berry-like cone, about ⅓ inch across, that grows on a very short stemlet or is connected directly to the branch. Cones are **bluish-white, with a waxy bloom**; they are usually profuse. When crushed, they **smell like gin.** (Male fruits are borne on separate plants; they are a short catkin rather than a round cone.) The cones are used as a seasoning.

SEASON: Fruits ripen in late summer, and usually persist through winter.

COMPARE: Creeping juniper (*J. horizontalis*) is a short shrub like common juniper, but its leaves are **scaly and overlapping**, growing **very close to the stem**; it is much less common in our area.

NOTES: True to its name, common juniper is the most widespread conifer in the world. It is native to the United States and Canada, as well as other areas as disparate as Eurasia, Japan, Croatia and Sweden; it typically grows as a columnar tree in areas other than North America, although the tree form is found in New England. The cones of common juniper are used to flavor gin.

green = key identification feature

LARGE
WOODY SHRUB

ALTERNATE
LEAVES

MID TO
LATE SUMMER

Pagoda Dogwood

Cornus alternifolia

HABITAT: Rich, mixed-wood and deciduous forests; rocky slopes; stream and swamp borders. Prefers moderate shade and well-drained soil.

GROWTH: A large native shrub that sometimes appears as a small tree, up to 25 feet tall with a flat-topped, spreading crown. Branches are tiered, with upturned ends; many grow **parallel to the ground**, giving the shrub a **layered appearance**. Young stems are greenish or reddish-purple; older bark is grayish-brown, with a rough, often furrowed texture.

LEAVES: Also called alternate-leaf dogwood, pagoda is the only dogwood with **alternate leaves**, which grow sparsely along the branches. At the ends of the branches, leaves grow in **whorled clusters**. Leaves are oval, tapering on both ends, with smooth edges, a sharp tip and long petiole (stemlet). Each leaf has **five or six pairs** of distinct veins that curve in towards the tip; the leaf surface is somewhat pillowy between the veins. Leaves are 2 to 5 inches long and one-half as wide; they are deep green and smooth above, paler and slightly hairy below.

FRUIT: Round, dark blue drupes, ¼ inch across, grow in flat, loose clusters at branch tips. The drupes are smooth and opaque, with a slight whitish bloom; stemlets are **bright coral-red**. The fruits are inedible.

SEASON: Fruits are greenish when young, gradually becoming reddish or lavender; they ripen fully in mid to late summer.

COMPARE: Round-leaved dogwood (*C. rugosa*) has **light blue** fruits on red stemlets; the leaves are **wider and rough** on the top, and stems are **green with purple blotches**. It is found in the same general areas as pagoda dogwood, although it is less common, particularly in Michigan. Silky dogwood (pg. 200) has blue fruits, but the stemlets are **dull purplish or greenish** rather than red; leaves have **three to five** pairs of shallow veins. Round-leaved and silky dogwood have **opposite** leaves, while those of pagoda dogwood are alternate.

NOTES: The fruits fall off or are eaten by wildlife fairly quickly, but the red stemlets remain, making an interesting display.

green = key identification feature

LARGE
WOODY SHRUB

OPPOSITE
LEAVES

MID TO
LATE SUMMER

Silky Dogwood

Cornus obliqua

HABITAT: Also known as swamp dogwood, due to its preference for wet sites. Grows on the edges of swamps, rivers and streams, in moist, rich, mixed-wood or deciduous forests, and also in seasonally flooded areas. Prefers shade or dappled sunlight.

GROWTH: A broad, open native shrub, up to 10 feet in height. Young stems are finely hairy (silky), and reddish or purplish with green tinges. Branches are smooth, with scattered pale lenticels (breathing pores); the trunk is grayish-brown and rough-textured, with shallow vertical fissures. Silky dogwood spreads by suckering, and may form wide colonies.

LEAVES: Leaves are oval, tapering on both ends, with a sharp tip; they grow oppositely on ½- to 1-inch petioles (stemlets). Each leaf has three to five pairs of shallow veins that curve in towards the tip; edges are untoothed and often slightly wavy. Leaves are 2 to 4 inches long and up to one-half as wide. They are medium green above, often tinged with red. Undersides are paler and often have a coating of very fine hair.

FRUIT: Round, smooth drupes, ⅓ inch across, grow in flat, loose clusters at branch tips; stemlets are dull purple or greenish. Immature fruits are pale, ripening to deep blue with metallic overtones. The fruits are inedible.

SEASON: Fruits ripen in mid to late summer.

COMPARE: *C. amomum*, also called silky dogwood, is extremely similar in appearance to *C. obliqua*; indeed, some references list *C. obliqua* as *C. amomum* ssp. *obliqua*. Leaves of *C. amomum* are usually wider, and have reddish hairs on the underside; in our area, *C. amomum* appears sporadically in Michigan. Several white-fruited dogwoods (pg. 260) have fruits that resemble immature silky dogwood fruits, but stems are not hairy and the fruits remain whitish. Round-leaved dogwood (*C. rugosa*) has light blue fruits, but fruit stemlets are red; leaves are much wider, and stems are green with purple blotches. Pagoda dogwood (pg. 198) has dark blue fruits on coral-red stemlets; leaves are alternate.

NOTES: *C. obliqua* is sometimes listed as pale dogwood.

green = key identification feature

Ripening berries

Bark of larger branch

LARGE
WOODY SHRUB

ALTERNATE
LEAVES

MID TO
LATE SUMMER

Highbush Blueberry

Vaccinium corymbosum

HABITAT: This native shrub is commonly cultivated, and many hybrids have been bred from it. In the wild, it is found in areas with acidic, moist soil and ample sunshine, including open woods, thickets and clearings. It tolerates damp ground and is often found in boggy or swampy areas.

GROWTH: This shrub usually has several main branches and numerous side branches; it can grow to 12 feet in height, although it is often shorter. Twigs are yellowish-green with small, raised brown dots; some twigs have a reddish tinge, and young stems turn red in winter. Older stems are brown, often with thin vertical furrows; the trunk has shreddy bark.

LEAVES: Alternate, oval leaves taper on both ends; edges are smooth or may have very fine teeth, and the tip is a slightly rounded point. Leaves are 1 to 2 inches long and about one-half as wide. They are deep green to bluish-green above; undersides are paler and often slightly hairy. Fall leaf color is spectacular, ranging from red to purple to orange.

FRUIT: Round berries with a prominent five-pointed crown on the bottom; when ripe, they are blue with a dusty bloom. Berries are ⅜ to ½ inch across, with small, soft seeds; they grow in clusters on short stemlets originating in leaf axils. Ripe berries are delicious raw or cooked. There are no toxic look-alikes with a five-pointed crown on the bottom.

SEASON: White urn-shaped flowers appear in mid to late spring. The berries that follow are green and hard at first, changing to pink before ripening to dusty blue in mid to late summer.

COMPARE: Lowbush, velvet-leaf and hillside blueberries (pg. 190) have fruits and leaves that resemble highbush blueberries, but their leaves are smaller and they are short shrubs that do not exceed 3 feet in height.

NOTES: Domesticated hybrids of this plant are the source for the blueberries sold in grocery stores. Wildlife such as birds, deer and small mammals enjoy the fruits almost as much as humans do.

green = key identification feature

LARGE
WOODY SHRUB

OPPOSITE
LEAVES

LATE
SUMMER

Withe-Rod

Viburnum nudum var. *cassinoides*

HABITAT: Moist areas, including swamps, bogs, and along ponds. Also found in openings in moist mixed-wood and coniferous forests and thickets.

GROWTH: An upright native shrub with a dense, rounded crown; generally 5 to 6 feet in height. Stems are brownish and slightly nubby in texture.

LEAVES: Roughly oval, tapering on both ends with a small, rounded point on the tip; 1½ to 3½ inches long and roughly one-half as wide. Opposite, on **short, round petioles** (stemlets). Leaves are smooth and firm-textured, almost leathery; tops are dark green, the undersides paler. Edges generally have fine teeth, and may be slightly wavy; some leaves have smooth edges. Young leaves are bronze in color. Leaves turn red or purplish in fall; often, the center or base of the leaf colors first, producing a splotchy appearance.

FRUIT: Oval drupes, about ⅜ inch long, grow in hanging, flat-topped clusters (cymes) on reddish stemlets at the ends of the branches. They are greenish-white when first formed, turning pink before ripening to deep blue or bluish-black with a dusty bloom; in late summer, **hot pink fruits are side-by-side with ripe, bluish-black fruits**, making a striking display. Fully ripe fruits develop a wrinkled texture. The fruits are edible, sweet and delicious. There are no toxic look-alikes.

SEASON: Fruits ripen in late summer; some persist into winter as wrinkled, dry blackish fruits that still make a tasty trail nibble.

COMPARE: Two plants in our area look quite similar. Nannyberries (pg. 246) have petioles with **flattened, wavy edges**; immature fruits are **reddish**, ripening to **black**. Possumhaw (*V. nudum*) has **lustrous** leaves up to **5 inches** long; immature fruits are **pink**, ripening to dark blue. In our area, possumhaw is found in Michigan and the northeastern part of Wisconsin.

NOTES: This plant is also called wild raisin, and listed as *V. cassinoides* in some texts. Its fruits have a modest amount of flesh in proportion to the pit; they make a great trail nibble, but for baking, the fruits need to be cooked and processed through a food mill to remove the pits.

green = key identification feature

204

TREE   OPPOSITE LEAVES   LATE SUMMER

Eastern Red Cedar

Juniperus virginiana

HABITAT: Rich, moist mixed-wood forests; abandoned agricultural areas; rocky outcrops and glades; pastures and clearings. Often found in areas with limestone; occasionally found in swampy areas.

GROWTH: A columnar native evergreen tree that can reach almost 100 feet in height but is usually 40 to 50 feet tall when found in the wild. Young twigs are greenish and scaly; branches are brownish-red. The oldest bark is shreddy, peeling off in long strips; exposed wood is gray. Eastern red cedar is generally unisexual—a plant is either male or female, and each produces a different type of fruit.

LEAVES: Two types of evergreen leaves grow on eastern red cedar. The primary type are tiny scales, which overlap so tightly on small twigs that the twigs appear to be four-sided, grayish-green scaly leaves. Young trees and new growth have pointed, awl-like needles, which are dark blue-green and about ½ inch long, growing in whorls of three. The foliage has a strong smell which is both piney and resinous.

FRUIT: The female fruit is an oblong, berry-like cone, about ¼ inch across, that grows at the tips of scale-covered branches. Cones are bluish, with a waxy bloom; they are usually profuse. (Male fruits are borne on separate plants; they look like small brown, tightly lapped "pine cones" growing at the ends of branches.) Female cones reportedly can be roasted to use as a coffee substitute, but are not edible.

SEASON: Fruits ripen in late summer, and usually persist through winter.

COMPARE: Creeping juniper (*J. horizontalis*) has scaly needles like those of eastern red cedar, but it grows as a short, spreading shrub; it is much less common in our area.

NOTES: Red cedar wood contains an oil that is a natural insect repellent. It is used to line chests (and make pencils), and also chipped for use as bedding for hamsters and other pet rodents. Fruits are eaten by waxwings, upland birds, and small mammals; the trees also provide nesting cover for birds.

green = key identification feature

NOT EDIBLE

TREE

ALTERNATE
LEAVES

LATE SUMMER
TO FALL

Sassafras

Sassafras albidum

HABITAT: This native tree is found in abandoned fields, open woodlands and forest openings, and along roads and fencerows; it often grows as a pioneer plant on disturbed sites. It produces suckers, and may form dense thickets. Sassafras grows best in sandy soil and partial shade, but will tolerate a range of soil types and full sun.

GROWTH: A medium-sized tree, 30 to 60 feet in height, with a broad, rounded crown. Twigs are smooth and yellowish-green; the trunk is reddish-brown and deeply furrowed, with flat-topped ridges. Sassafras trees are unisexual—a tree is either male or female, and each produces a different type of flower and fruit.

LEAVES: Three shapes grow on sassafras trees. Some are oval, but the most characteristic leaves have two or three lobes with deep sinuses (the curved depression between the lobes). The lobes are not symmetrical on two-lobed leaves, so the leaf resembles a mitten; three-lobed leaves are fairly symmetrical. Leaves are 3 to 7 inches long and about two-thirds as wide; edges are smooth, and the base is sharply tapered. The leaves grow alternately on long, reddish petioles (stemlets); they are bright green above, and white beneath. Trees growing in alkaline soil have yellowish-green leaves with darker areas around the veins. In fall, the leaves turn yellow, orange or scarlet.

FRUIT: Oval, deep-blue drupes, about ½ inch long, grow singly or in clusters on long, curved red stalks at the branch tips of female trees. The top of the stalk, at the base of the fruit, is swollen and cup-like. The fruits are inedible.

SEASON: Fruits mature in late summer to fall.

COMPARE: Mulberries (pg. 152) have some mitten-like leaves, but the leaves are toothy and the fruits are compound drupes.

NOTES: All parts of the plant have a spicy scent, and were used medicinally by American Indians and pioneers. Ground dried leaves are sold as filé, a powder used to thicken gumbo; root bark is used to brew tea.

green = key identification feature

TREE

ALTERNATE
LEAVES

LATE SUMMER
TO FALL

Blackgum –OR– Tupelo

Nyssa sylvatica

HABITAT: This native tree thrives in areas with rich, moist soil, but also grows in dry, rocky areas. It is found next to streams and ponds, in swampy areas and creek bottoms, and in openings in damp woodlands. It prefers full sun and is tolerant of seasonal flooding.

GROWTH: A medium to large tree, often 60 to 80 feet in height, with dense foliage and a pyramidal crown. The trunk, which may be up to 3 feet thick, is straight, and branches are horizontal or slightly drooping. Branches are smooth and gray or reddish, with small lenticels (breathing pores); the trunk is dark grayish-brown, with irregular, flat ridges.

LEAVES: Glossy, leathery oval leaves, 4 to 6 inches long and one-half as wide, grow alternately on short petioles (stemlets); leaves often cluster on short spur branches along the main branch. They are deep green on top, yellowish-green underneath. Edges are smooth, but some leaves have several very large teeth that look like pointed lobes. Leaf bases may be rounded or tapered; tips come to a blunt point. The leaves turn brilliant scarlet, orange or purplish in fall.

FRUIT: Round to oval drupes, about ½ inch long, grow singly or in small clusters on long, thin stemlets along side branches; ripe fruits are dark blue with a dusty bloom. They contain a single, large pit; the flesh is thin but juicy, with a bitter flavor reminiscent of lime peels. The fruits can be eaten in the field as an astringent refresher; according to some reports, they can also be used to make preserves.

SEASON: Fruits ripen in late summer to fall.

COMPARE: The related water tupelo (*N. aquatica*) is similar, but its trunk flares out at the base; it grows in swampy areas. It is found in the southeastern quarter of the U.S. and does not grow in our area.

NOTES: Birds devour the fruit very quickly upon its ripening. Honey made by bees feeding on tupelo flowers is very highly regarded.

green = key identification feature

TENDER
LEAFY PLANT

WHORLED
COMPOUND
LEAVES

SUMMER

Sarsaparilla

Aralia nudicaulis

HABITAT: Rich, moist, sun-dappled mixed-wood and hardwood forests; thickets and prairie areas; occasionally near streams and bogs.

GROWTH: This native plant has a whorl of three compound leaves at the top of a long, erect **hairless** leaf stalk that grows from the underground rhizome (root-bearing stem); the total plant height may be as much as 2 feet, but it is usually shorter. The **flowering/fruiting stalk is separate**, rising from the same point as the leaf stalk; it is shorter, typically 5 to 8 inches in height.

LEAVES: Three compound leaves grow in a whorl; each of the three leaf stalks has three to five (sometimes seven) oval, toothy leaflets with rounded bases and pointed tips. Leaflets are 2 to 5 inches long and about two-thirds as wide; they often have wavy edges.

FRUIT: The leafless fruiting stalk divides into **three stemlets** (occasionally two); each is topped with a **rounded cluster of black berries on slender stemlets** that emanate from a central point, much like the fluffy head of a dandelion gone to seed. Berries are round, and about ⅛ inch in diameter. They are inedible when raw; although they may be edible when cooked, sources disagree on this, so they are best left to the birds, foxes and bears, who consume them with no ill effects.

SEASON: Fruits ripen in midsummer.

COMPARE: With its distinctive whorl of three compound leaves and separate fruiting stalk topped with ball-shaped berry clusters, sarsaparilla really doesn't resemble anything else in the woods.

NOTES: The underground rhizome is very fragrant, and has been used to make tea and other beverages. It is not, however, the source of the flavoring in root beer and the soft drink called sarsaparilla; rather, that flavor traditionally came from the roots and bark of the unrelated sassafras tree (pg. 208).

green = key identification feature

TENDER
LEAFY PLANT

ALTERNATE
LEAVES

LATE
SUMMER

American Pokeweed
Phytolacca americana

HABITAT: Agricultural areas, waste ground, fencelines, railroad beds, field edges, shelterbelts, disturbed sites. Requires adequate moisture; can grow in sun or shade.

GROWTH: An upright, multi-branching leafy native plant, up to 12 feet in height but generally much shorter. Stems are green when young, turning reddish or purplish as they mature. The central stem often becomes quite thick, up to 1 inch in diameter.

LEAVES: Alternate, oblong leaves, up to 12 inches long and roughly one-third as wide. The base of leaf tapers into the long petiole (stemlet); the leaf is broadest at the midpoint, tapering to a point at the tip. Leaves are bright green and coarsely textured with smooth edges; they have an unpleasant scent when crushed.

FRUIT: The most distinctive part of the plant. Shiny, purplish-black berries with an indent in the bottom, each ¼ to ⅓ inch wide and often slightly flattened, grow in a raceme (a long fruit cluster) from hot-pink stemlets; the hanging fruit stem is also hot pink, and up to 15 inches in length. The berries are poisonous, containing toxic alkaloids.

SEASON: Berries develop in early to midsummer; they are green at first, turning white with white stemlets, before ripening in late summer.

COMPARE: When it is fruiting, pokeweed is hard to miss, or to confuse with other plants. The dark berries on the hot-pink stem, combined with the overall size of the plant and its leaves, make this plant easy to identify.

NOTES: Although *all parts of the pokeweed plant contain deadly, toxic alkaloids,* young shoots of pokeweed are traditionally eaten as a cooked green, especially in the South; special preparations are needed to eliminate the toxic constituents. Sap from the plant can cause an allergic reaction in sensitive individuals. The berries can be used to produce ink and a red dye; according to some sources, the juice was used in the past to intensify the color of cheap wine.

green = key identification feature

TENDER
LEAFY PLANT

ALTERNATE
LEAVES

LATE SUMMER
TO EARLY FALL

Eastern Black Nightshade
Solanum ptycanthum

HABITAT: Agricultural areas, waste ground, urban areas, thickets, woodland openings, rocky ground and vacant lots. It does best in partial to full sun, and can adapt to moist or dry conditions.

GROWTH: A tender, branching native annual, up to 3 feet in height but often shorter. Stems are green and round when young, often with scattered hairs; they become brownish, angular and woody over the season.

LEAVES: Alternate, slightly hairy on both surfaces. Purplish when young changing to deep green, although undersides are typically tinged with purple even on mature leaves. The shape is inconsistent; in general, they are broadly triangular to elliptic, but edges may be smooth and wavy, or may have wide, blunt teeth. Larger leaves are up to 3 inches in length and two-thirds as wide, although the plant typically has numerous smaller leaves near the ends of the branches.

FRUIT: Round berries, about ⅓ inch in diameter with a star-shaped cap, grow in hanging clusters of five to seven. Berries are hard and green when young, softening and ripening to a deep, glossy black; they have juicy pulp and numerous flat seeds. Underripe berries are toxic. Some foragers eat fully ripe berries, in small quantities, but it is tricky to judge ripeness accurately, and even ripe berries cause intestinal problems in some people. It's best to avoid them entirely.

SEASON: Black nightshade produces small, white, star-shaped flowers throughout the summer; the berries follow, ripening continuously from late summer through early fall.

COMPARE: Climbing nightshade (pg. 100) grows as a vine; its fruits are red when ripe. Two other non-vining nightshades occasionally grow in our area. Berries of cutleaf nightshade (*S. triflorum*) are orange when ripe; those of hoe nightshade (*S. physalifolium*) are yellowish-green.

NOTES: Also spelled *S. ptychanthum*. Sometimes listed as a synonym for black nightshade (*S. nigrum*); however, according to the USDA Plants Database, *S. nigrum* is a separate species that does not grow here.

green = key identification feature

Toxic when
underripe

VINING
PLANT

ALTERNATE
LEAVES

LATE
SUMMER

•see below

Smilax

Smilax spp.

HABITAT: These native vines are found in openings in moist, rich deciduous forests; thickets, clearings, and waste ground; and along streambanks.

GROWTH: *Smilax* is a family of vining plants, growing up to 10 feet long; some have tendrils which they use to climb over other plants, while others lack tendrils and simply recline over other plants when they become too tall to support themselves. There are two types of *Smilax*: non-woody (in our area, these are common carrion-flower, *Smilax lasioneura;* upright carrion-flower, *S. ecirrhata;* smooth carrion-flower, *S. herbacea;* and Illinois greenbrier, *S. illinoensis*) and woody (in our area, catbrier, *S. rotundifolia;* and bristly greenbrier, *S. tamnoides*). The woody species are armed with bristles and, sometimes, thorns.

LEAVES: *Smilax* in our area have broadly oval or heart-shaped leaves, with several deep parallel veins that have a web of smaller veins between them. Leaves grow alternately along the stem; they are generally 3 to 5 inches long and one-half to three-quarters as wide.

FRUIT: Both woody and non-woody *Smilax* produce similar rounded or ball-shaped clusters of berries on long, stiff stalks. Fruits of all *Smilax* in our area are dark bluish-black with a whitish bloom (a few species found in the southern states have red berries). The fruits are generally considered edible, but most are reportedly rubbery and distasteful.

SEASON: Berries ripen in late summer, and may persist into winter.

COMPARE: The berry cluster may be mistaken for wild grapes (pg. 170); however, the leaf structure and stalk on *Smilax* make identification easy.

NOTES: Shoots of the non-woody species noted above are a prime spring-time wild edible (*The Forager's Harvest*, Sam Thayer). The non-woody species are often collectively called "carrion flower" because some of them produce flowers with a highly unpleasant smell. For information that helps identify the various *Smilax* species in our area, please visit the website of the Robert W. Freckmann Herbarium (University of Wisconsin, Stevens Point) at http://wisflora.herbarium.wisc.edu/.

green = key identification feature

* combined range

Common carrion-flower

Lower stem of bristly greenbrier

NOT EDIBLE

WOODY
VINE

OPPOSITE
LEAVES

LATE SUMMER
TO FALL

Japanese Honeysuckle

Lonicera japonica

HABITAT: This non-native vine has escaped from cultivation, and is increasingly found in a wide variety of habitats, including agricultural areas, thickets, woodlands, disturbed areas and alongside roads and railroads. It tolerates shade, but also grows in sunny areas.

GROWTH: A trailing or climbing vine, typically less than 10 feet in length but sometimes longer; it grows compactly and so profusely that it often resembles a shrub from a distance. It has **no tendrils**, and climbs by twining itself around poles, fences, trees and other plants; it can girdle and kill trees with its twining stems. It often forms **dense canopies** in forested areas. Young stems are reddish-brown and hairy; older stems and the trunk are tan, with **shreddy bark**.

LEAVES: Oval leaves, 1 to 3 inches in length and one-half to two-thirds as wide, grow oppositely on short petioles (stemlets). Leaf bases are broad; the tip is often pointed, but may also be rounded. Top sides are bright green, often with fine hairs but sometimes almost smooth; undersides are paler, with hairs along the main vein. **Leaves remain green and on the plant** until the temperatures drop well below freezing; in protected areas, they may remain through winter.

FRUIT: Round to oval berries, about ¼ inch long, grow **singly or in pairs on stubby stalks** from leaf axils. Berries are juicy, and contain two or more small seeds; they are glossy black when ripe. They are inedible.

SEASON: Fragrant whitish flowers are present in late spring, turning yellow with age. Berries follow, ripening to black in late summer to fall.

COMPARE: Several native honeysuckle **vines** grow in our area, but ripe fruits are red, and the **leaves at the tip of the stem fuse to form a cup**; please see pg. 102 for more information.

NOTES: Japanese honeysuckle is native to Asia; it was brought to this country in the early 1800s as an ornamental and for erosion control. It is considered a noxious, invasive plant due to its rapid, dense growth, which often shades out native plants.

green = key identification feature

SMALL
WOODY SHRUB

ALTERNATE
COMPOUND
LEAVES

SUMMER

Black Raspberry

Rubus occidentalis

HABITAT: Disturbed areas, especially those that have been logged or cut. Also found in tangled meadows, along streams and lakes, next to trails or roads, and in open woods. This native plant grows in both shady and sunny areas, but produces more fruit in moderate to full sun.

GROWTH: Black raspberries are brambles, sprawling vine-like shrubs that often form a thicket. Stems, called canes, grow to 6 feet in length, and usually arch but may also be upright. Black raspberry canes have sharp, curved thorns. Young canes are unbranched and have a whitish bloom that can be rubbed off; older canes are branched and purplish.

LEAVES: The compound leaves grow alternately on long, smooth petioles (stemlets). Leaves usually have three leaflets, occasionally five. The terminal leaflet has a long petiole; side leaflets attach directly to the stem. Leaflets have doubly toothed edges, with a sharply pointed tip and a rounded base; they are up to 3 inches long, and whitish below.

FRUIT: A compound drupe, up to ½ inch across. Fruits are green and hard at first, progressing through several color changes and becoming yellowish, salmon-colored, bright red, purplish-red, and finally ripening to purplish-black. Ripe fruits detach cleanly from the plant, leaving the receptacle (core) behind; the picked fruit is hollow. Fruits are edible and delicious. When the fruits are ripe, there are no toxic look-alikes.

SEASON: Black raspberries ripen in early to midsummer, generally before red raspberries (pg. 116) and well before blackberries (pg. 234).

COMPARE: Underripe black raspberries look like red raspberries; however, red raspberry canes are prickly but not thorny and lack the whitish bloom. If you find raspberries that are red but hard and won't detach from the receptacle (core) easily, you've found underripe black raspberries. Blackberries have similar growth habits and a black compound fruit, but stems are ridged and have no bloom; picked fruit is not hollow.

NOTES: Black raspberries are considered by many to be the tastiest berry in the *Rubus* genus (which includes raspberries and blackberries).

green = key identification feature

SMALL
WOODY SHRUB

ALTERNATE
LEAVES

MID TO
LATE SUMMER

Sand Cherry

Prunus pumila

HABITAT: Open dunes; sandy or gravelly shorelines of lakes and rivers; sandy or rocky edges of coniferous forests; grassy prairie areas. Sand cherry prefers sunny areas and tolerates dry conditions; it can survive harsh winters.

GROWTH: A sparse, low native shrub, 2 to 9 feet in height, with upright branches. In windy areas, it may recline rather than stand upright. Twigs are reddish; branches are reddish-brown, becoming gray with age. Bark is marked with light-colored lenticels (breathing pores).

LEAVES: Narrowly oval, tapering on both ends, with a leathery texture; they grow alternately from the stems on petioles (stemlets) that are often reddish. Leaves are 1 to 2 inches in length and roughly one-third as wide; edges have scattered small teeth, especially toward the tip. Deep green and glossy on top, lighter beneath; tips and leaf edges sometimes have a reddish tinge.

FRUIT: An oval drupe with a single pit; it is about 1 inch long and glossy black when ripe. There is more flesh in proportion to the pit than on chokecherries (pg. 136) or pin cherries (pg. 156). Fruits are edible; they are sweet but somewhat astringent. They are usually cooked to make jam or preserves. There are no toxic look-alikes.

SEASON: Fruits ripen from mid to late summer.

COMPARE: With its inch-long glossy black fruit and leathery and oval leaves on reddish petioles, sand cherry doesn't resemble anything else in our area when it is fruiting.

NOTES: The deep roots of sand cherry help stabilize sand dunes around the Great Lakes. The fruit is eaten by large birds; the twigs are browsed by deer and small mammals. Birds use the shrubs for nesting and escape cover. Sand cherry leaves, stems and pits contain hydrocyanic acid, a cyanide-producing compound. The leaves and pits should never be eaten, and care should be taken to avoid crushing the pits when juicing the fruits. Cooking or drying eliminates the harmful compound.

green = key identification feature

SMALL
WOODY SHRUB

ALTERNATE
LEAVES

MID TO
LATE SUMMER

Missouri

Northern

Blackish Gooseberries

Ribes spp.

HABITAT: Two native gooseberry shrubs with blackish fruits grow in our area. Missouri gooseberry (*Ribes missouriense*) grows in open woodlands, thickets, fields and floodplains. Northern or Canadian gooseberry (*R. oxyacanthoides*) is found in moist woods, thickets and on rocky shorelines. The ranges of the two species are almost mutually exclusive.

GROWTH: Both are arching shrubs; stems of the Missouri species may be up to 6 feet long, while those of northern gooseberry are 4 feet or less. Both have one to three long, sharp thorns at leaf nodes, and many thin bristles on the lower parts of the stems; young stems of both species may have few to no bristles. Missouri gooseberry thorns are typically reddish-brown.

LEAVES: Attached alternately to the stem by a petiole (stemlet); leaf nodes have up to three leaves. Each leaf has three to five lobes, resembling a rounded maple leaf. Missouri gooseberry leaves are shallowly lobed, with rounded teeth, and the leaf bases are often wedge-shaped, but may also be flat. Northern gooseberry leaves have lobes that are more deeply divided, and the bases are frequently straight to heart-shaped.

FRUIT: The ¼- to ½-inch round berry grows on a thin stemlet from leaf nodes, singly or in small clusters. Distinct stripes run longitudinally on the berry; a long flower remnant, often called a pigtail, is present at the end of the berry. Berries of both species listed here are dark reddish-purple to blackish-purple. They are edible in both the green and ripe stages.

SEASON: Ripe fruits are present from mid to late summer.

COMPARE: Fruits of prickly and swamp gooseberries (pg. 174) are reddish-purple when ripe; stems of both have moderate to sparse bristles. Currant shrubs (pgs. 120, 228) resemble gooseberry shrubs, but berries are smaller and grow in long, hanging clusters of multiple fruits.

NOTES: Ripe gooseberries are excellent in baked desserts, sauces and other dishes. Green gooseberries (pg. 46) are used for jam and jelly. You don't have to wait for gooseberries to ripen fully before picking, since they are edible even when green (as long as they are soft).

green = key identification feature

DELICIOUS

Missouri gooseberry

Northern gooseberry

SMALL
WOODY SHRUB

ALTERNATE
LEAVES

MID TO
LATE SUMMER

*see below

Black Currants

Ribes spp.

HABITAT: Four varieties of native black currant inhabit our region. American black currant (*Ribes americanum*, pictured at right) is the most common. Northern black currant (*R. hudsonianum*) and bristly black currant (*R. lacustre*) are found in our area primarily in the north. Golden currant (*R. aureum*), common in the western U.S., is scattered in just a few counties in each state in our area. All inhabit moist woodlands, swampy areas, parklands and streambanks.

GROWTH: A straggling shrub, generally 3 to 6 feet in height, that often clambers over other plants; golden currant can reach 9 feet in height. Bristly black currant has bristly stems, and thorns at the leaf nodes; all other currants listed here have smooth stems and are thornless.

LEAVES: Attached alternately to the stem by a thin petiole (stemlet). Each leaf has three to five distinct lobes, resembling a small, roughly textured maple leaf. Leaves of American black currant have tiny golden resin dots on both surfaces (visible with a lens); those of northern black currant have resin dots on the underside only. When crushed, leaves of northern black currant and bristly black currant emit an unpleasant odor.

FRUIT: Round ¼- to ⅜-inch berries grow in a raceme (a long cluster of multiple fruits). Immature berries are green, turning red before ripening to black. Berries of bristly black currant have numerous gland-tipped hairs, while those of northern black currant are smooth but covered in resin dots; both are unpalatable but can be eaten safely. Berries of the other currants listed here are delicious, and can be eaten raw, used in baking, or cooked into jelly and other dishes. There are no toxic look-alikes.

SEASON: Black currants ripen in mid to late summer.

COMPARE: Gooseberries (pgs. 46, 174, 226) and red currants (pg. 120) have similar leaves and growth habits, but most gooseberry plants have thorns at some or all leaf nodes. Gooseberry fruits grow in clusters of two or three, in contrast to currants, which grow in a raceme.

NOTES: Golden currant, also called clove currant, has a clove-like odor.

green = key identification feature   * combined range

American black currant

SMALL
WOODY SHRUB

ALTERNATE
LEAVES

MID TO
LATE SUMMER

Black Huckleberry

Gaylussacia baccata

HABITAT: This native plant is found in dry habitats, including rocky or sandy areas, open mixed-wood forests and thickets.

GROWTH: A low, upright, multi-stemmed shrub, up to 3 feet in height but usually shorter; often grows in colonies. Branches are yellowish-green to reddish-brown; older stems are gray.

LEAVES: Alternate, roughly oval, tapering at both ends; the tip may be somewhat rounded on some leaves. Bright green and slightly glossy on top, yellowish beneath, with a profusion of tiny yellow resin dots (visible with a lens) on the underside. Leaves are 1 to 2 inches long and one-half as wide; edges are smooth. They grow on a short, hairy petiole (stemlet).

FRUIT: The round berry has a prominent five-pointed crown on the bottom; when ripe, it is blackish-blue. Berries are typically ¼ to ⅓ inch across, and have greenish flesh with 10 small seeds that are small but fairly hard. They grow on short racemes (clusters of multiple fruits) originating in the leaf axils. Ripe huckleberries are delicious raw or cooked. There are no toxic look-alikes.

SEASON: Berries ripen in mid to late summer.

COMPARE: Huckleberries may be mistaken for blueberries (pgs. 190, 202) or bilberries (pg. 192); however, ripe fruits of these plants are blue with a whitish bloom, and their leaves lack the resin dots found on huckleberry leaves. Both are edible; their seeds are smaller and softer than those of the huckleberry.

NOTES: Huckleberries and blueberries often grow in the same places. Distinguishing between the two is more a matter of curiosity than of necessity, because they can be used in exactly the same manner as one another for cooking or eating out-of-hand. In many places, the word "huckleberry" is used to refer to members of the *Vaccinium* genus, which includes blueberries.

green = key identification feature

Resin dots
on underside

SMALL
WOODY SHRUB

ALTERNATE
COMPOUND
LEAVES

MID TO
LATE SUMMER

Common Dewberry

Rubus flagellaris

HABITAT: This native plant, also called northern dewberry, inhabits open forests and thickets; it is also found along streambanks and roads. It will tolerate partial sun, but produces more fruit in full sun.

GROWTH: A trailing, low-growing shrub that may appear vine-like. Stems (canes) are woody but weak, usually sprawling along the ground rather than rising erect; the tips often develop roots. They have scattered curved prickles along the stem. Young stems are greenish, becoming brownish and woody in their second year.

LEAVES: Compound, doubly toothy leaves grow alternately on the stems, on long petioles (stemlets) that are usually hairy or prickly; there are two leaf-like stipules at the base of the leaf stalk where it joins the stem. Leaves of fruiting canes typically have three leaflets. Each leaflet is up to 3 inches in length and one-third as wide, with a tapered or wedge-shaped base. The central leaflet has a short petiole (stemlet); side leaflets are attached directly to the stem.

FRUIT: The compound drupe, ½ to ¾ inch long, resembles a small blackberry; like blackberries, the receptacle (core) usually remains inside the picked fruit. Dewberry fruits are green and hard at first, turning red before ripening to glossy black. Fruits are edible and usually quite tasty; quality varies from plant to plant. When dewberries are ripe, there are no toxic look-alikes.

SEASON: Dewberries ripen from mid to late summer.

COMPARE: Numerous varieties of black dewberries inhabit our region; the differences between species are fairly subtle, and all are edible. Some dewberries have fruits that are red when ripe; please see pg. 84 for information on these. Blackberries (pg. 234) have similar fruits which are black when ripe, but they are an arching or upright shrub. Red and black raspberries (pg. 116, 222) have similar leaves, but grow as arching brambles several feet long; fruits are hollow when picked.

NOTES: Dewberries grow low to the ground, often underneath other plants.

green = key identification feature

SMALL
WOODY SHRUB

ALTERNATE
COMPOUND
LEAVES

LATE
SUMMER

Blackberries

Rubus allegheniensis and others

HABITAT: Scrubby areas, waste ground, pastures, sun-dappled woods, forest clearings and thickets; also found alongside paths and roads.

GROWTH: Blackberries are brambles, sprawling vine-like shrubs that may form a thicket. Stems, called canes, can be 8 feet or more in length, and are usually arching but may be upright. Blackberry canes are ridged, and star-shaped in cross-section, with sharp thorns that are often curved. Young canes are generally reddish or greenish, with no whitish bloom; older canes are brownish. More than a dozen native blackberry varieties grow in our area; the Allegheny blackberry, *Rubus allegheniensis*, is the most common. Some have fewer thorns; they may have smaller leaves or longer fruit clusters, and the depth of the teeth on the leaves varies. All produce edible fruit; exact identification is a matter for botanists.

LEAVES: Compound, doubly toothy, coarsely textured leaves with long petioles (stemlets) are attached alternately to the canes; undersides are pale. Leaves of fruiting canes have three leaflets; non-fruiting canes typically have five leaflets. Leaflet size varies between species; most are up to 5 inches long, and the terminal leaflet is often larger than side leaflets.

FRUIT: A compound drupe, about ½ inch across and often somewhat longer. Fruits are green and hard at first, turning red before ripening to glossy black. The receptacle (core) remains inside the picked berry so the fruit is solid, not hollow like a raspberry. Blackberries are edible raw or cooked; there are no toxic look-alikes with black fruits in our area.

SEASON: Blackberries are red and underripe in early summer; they ripen in mid to late summer, well after red raspberries (pg. 116) and black raspberries (pg. 222).

COMPARE: Several other *Rubus* in our area have black compound drupes. Black raspberries (pg. 222) are hollow when picked; stems are round, with a whitish bloom on young growth. Dewberries (pgs. 84, 232) are low-growing, vine-like plants rather than arching or upright shrubs.

NOTES: Blackberries have larger, coarser seeds than other brambles.

green = key identification feature

SMALL
WOODY SHRUB

ALTERNATE
LEAVES

EARLY FALL

Alder-Leaved Buckthorn

Rhamnus alnifolia

HABITAT: Moist areas, including mixed-wood forests, damp meadows, swampy areas, streambanks and thickets. Sometimes found growing on the wet edge of a pond or lake.

GROWTH: A short, upright native shrub, 3 feet or less in height and equal spread. Branches fork several times. Twigs are smooth and reddish or brownish; young branches are downy. It may form colonies, with many short shrubs in a tight group. Alder-leaved buckthorn is usually unisexual—a plant is either male or female, and each produces a different type of flower and fruit. Flowers of alder-leaved buckthorn are greenish and inconspicuous.

LEAVES: Roughly oval, with a sharp tip; each has five to eight pairs of deep, gently curving veins. Leaves are up to 4 inches in length and one-half as wide; they grow alternately from the stems on short, smooth petioles (stemlets). Edges are finely toothed; the top surface is smooth and somewhat glossy, and the underside may be slightly hairy, although it is also somewhat glossy. Tiny paired, leaf-like appendages called stipules grow at the base of each leaf petiole.

FRUIT: Glossy round drupes, about ⅓ inch in diameter, are red when under-ripe, turning black when ripe; they may appear slightly lobed. Fruits grow on thin stemlets from the leaf axils. They are inedible.

SEASON: Fruits are red in late summer, turning black by early fall.

COMPARE: Common buckthorn (pg. 244) is much taller, and is found in drier habitat; its leaves are more egg-shaped. Glossy buckthorn (pg. 130) is also much taller; it has smooth-edged leaves that are typically alternate but may be opposite, and leaf undersides are hairy.

NOTES: Unlike common buckthorn and glossy buckthorn, alder-leaved buckthorn is a native plant; it is not considered invasive, and can sometimes be hard to find.

green = key identification feature

LARGE
WOODY SHRUB

OPPOSITE
LEAVES

MID TO
LATE SUMMER

Downy Arrowwood

Viburnum rafinesquianum

HABITAT: Dry mixed-wood and hardwood forests. Downy arrowwood is drought-tolerant, and very adaptable.

GROWTH: An open, multi-branched native shrub with a rounded top, generally 6 to 8 feet in height and slightly less wide. Branches are erect and straight, spreading outward from the base. The bark is smooth and dark gray; unlike other *Viburnums*, the bark does not become flaky with age.

LEAVES: Opposite, dark green leaves with 10 or fewer pairs of large teeth grow on short, hairy petioles (stemlets); leaves are 1½ to 3 inches in length and one-third to one-half as wide. Leaves are broadest below the midpoint, with a rounded base; they taper to the softly pointed tip. Leaf edges have very fine hairs (visible with a lens); undersides are hairy (particularly on the veins) and light green. Foliage turns rosy maroon in the fall.

FRUIT: Oval to round drupes, each about ½ inch long, grow in open, flat-topped clusters at the ends of branches; fruit stalks are yellowish to reddish. Fruits are yellowish-green, turning blue, then ripening to shiny bluish-black. The fruits are very bitter, with thin flesh in proportion to the pits, and are generally regarded as inedible.

SEASON: Downy arrowwood produces flat-topped clusters of showy white flowers, which smell unpleasant, in early summer. Fruits ripen in mid to late summer.

COMPARE: Nannyberry (pg. 246) produces similar clusters of black fruit, but the leaves are up to 5 inches long, with fine teeth; the petioles are flattened, with wavy edges.

NOTES: Wood from this species was used to make arrows, because the branches are long and straight, with no tapering. Fruits of downy arrowwood were reportedly eaten by American Indian peoples in Canada (*Traditional Plant Foods of Canadian Indigenous Peoples*, Harriet V. Kuhnlein and Nancy J. Turner).

green = key identification feature

LARGE
WOODY SHRUB

ALTERNATE
LEAVES

LATE SUMMER
TO EARLY FALL

Black

Purple

Chokeberries –or– Aronia

Aronia spp.

HABITAT: Two species of this plant are native to our area: black chokeberry (*Aronia melanocarpa*; also listed as *Photinia melanocarpa*) and purple chokeberry (*A. prunifolia*). The purple species is sometimes considered a naturally occurring hybrid between black and red chokeberries (*A. arbutifolia*, a species found in the southeastern and eastern U.S. but not in our area); other sources list it as a distinct species. Both inhabit moist thickets, wetlands and forest openings, and occasionally dry areas.

GROWTH: A leggy shrub; purple chokeberries may be up to 12 feet in height, while the black species is generally shorter. Young stems are reddish-brown; older stems have noticeable lenticels (breathing pores). Chokeberries produce suckers (shoots) and may form thickets.

LEAVES: Glossy, bright green leaves with finely toothed edges are 2 to 3 inches long and oval, broadest at or above the midpoint; the tip often comes to a sharp point, and edges of the teeth have small glands (visible with a hand lens). Leaves grow alternately on short petioles (stemlets) that are often reddish. The base of the midribs on the top side have small dark, hair-like glands (visible with a lens). Leaf undersides are pale. Leaves turn red in fall.

FRUIT: A glossy, round pome; fruits of black chokeberries are black when ripe, while those of purple chokeberry are purplish-black to purplish. The bottom has distinct indentations in a star pattern; it looks a bit like a pucker. Fruits are about ⅓ inch in diameter, and grow in small clusters on long, thin stemlets at the ends of branches. The fruit is acrid but tasty when sweetened; its seeds are so soft that they are unnoticeable.

SEASON: Fruits ripen in late summer to early fall, and may persist on the plant through winter.

COMPARE: Buckthorn fruits (pgs. 130, 236, 244) are black with no pucker on the bottom; fruits grow from leaf axils rather than at branch tips.

NOTES: Aronia juice is popular in Europe and often found at health-food markets in the U.S. Chokeberries are often planted for landscaping.

green = key identification feature

Black chokeberry

LARGE
WOODY SHRUB

OPPOSITE
LEAVES

LATE SUMMER
TO EARLY FALL

Mapleleaf Viburnum

Viburnum acerifolium

HABITAT: This native shrub, also called dockmackie, is a common under-story plant in open woodlands, particularly beech-maple forests; it also grows on hillsides and alongside ravines. It prefers dappled shade and moist, well-drained soil, but grows well in deep shade and dry conditions.

GROWTH: A somewhat sparse shrub up to 6 feet in height, mapleleaf viburnum readily develops suckers and forms thickets. Twigs are downy and brownish; the trunk is smooth and grayish, often with pale blotches.

LEAVES: Mapleleaf viburnum has **several types of leaves**; all grow oppositely on downy, ½- to ¾-inch petioles (stemlets). Some leaves are shaped like maple leaves, with three distinct lobes; others have indistinct lobes and are heart-shaped, while a few are oval in shape with no lobes at all. Most are 2½ to 4 inches in length and width, although some are smaller. All have deep veins; the top sides are deep green, while the undersides are paler and hairy, with tiny **black dots**. Most have coarse, sharp teeth all around except on the base, which may be rounded or notched; the tip is sharply pointed. In fall, the leaves turn reddish to purplish.

FRUIT: Egg-shaped drupes, ½ inch long, grow on thin stemlets in clusters on stalks that grow from the branch tips, beyond the last pair of leaves. Fruits are green, turning reddish before ripening to **black**. They are inedible.

SEASON: Clusters of yellowish-white flowers appear in early summer. The fruit is present much of the summer, ripening in late summer to early fall; it may persist over winter if not eaten by wildlife.

COMPARE: Because of its leaf shape, mapleleaf viburnum may be mistaken for a maple, particularly mountain maple (*Acer spicatum*), a **shrub-like** maple; however, maple fruits are **dry, flat seeds with propeller-like wings**. Highbush cranberry and guelder rose (pg. 142) also have maple-like leaves, but they are much leafier plants that are usually **taller**, and their ripe fruits are **red**.

NOTES: Thickets of mapleleaf viburnum provide food, as well as good nest-ing and escape cover for numerous species of birds and small mammals.

green = key identification feature

LARGE
WOODY SHRUB

OPPOSITE
LEAVES

LATE SUMMER
TO EARLY FALL

Common Buckthorn
Rhamnus cathartica

HABITAT: Open hardwood forests, prairie areas, fields, forest edges, urban parks, shelterbelts, floodplains, ravines and fencerows. Prefers partial shade, and can tolerate moist or dry conditions.

GROWTH: A large, multi-stemmed shrub with a spreading crown, sometimes appearing to be a small tree; up to 20 feet in height but usually much shorter. Bark is gray to brown; older stems are roughly textured, with long, corky protrusions. Twigs often have a spine at the tip, giving the species its common name.

LEAVES: Dark, glossy green, broadly oval, with a pointed tip and a broad base; leaves grow oppositely on long petioles (stemlets). Leaves are 1½ to 3 inches long, and roughly two-thirds as wide; both surfaces are hairless. Edges are finely toothy; each leaf has three to five pairs of deep veins that curve in toward the tip to follow the edge of the leaf. Leaves remain green late into fall, long after most other shrubs have lost their leaves.

FRUIT: Glossy, round black drupes, about ¼ inch in diameter, grow on thin stemlets in dense clusters at leaf axils, or singly along the stems. The fruits are strongly cathartic, and are considered toxic.

SEASON: Common buckthorn ripens in late summer to early fall.

COMPARE: Glossy buckthorn (pg. 130) has smooth-edged leaves that are typically alternate; leaf undersides are hairy, and the twigs are lacking the spine at the tip. Alder-leaved buckthorn (pg. 236) is short, 3 feet or less; it grows in wetter areas, and its leaves are narrower. Many dogwood species (pgs. 158, 198, 200, 260) have leaves with similar veins, but the fruits are borne in clusters at branch tips.

NOTES: Common buckthorn is a non-native species, imported in the late 1800s from Europe for use as a landscape plant. It has naturalized, and is considered invasive throughout most of its range. It spreads rapidly, crowding out native plants.

green = key identification feature

LARGE SHRUB
OR SMALL TREE

OPPOSITE
LEAVES

LATE SUMMER
TO EARLY FALL

Nannyberry

Viburnum lentago

HABITAT: Openings and edges in moist, well-drained hardwood and mixed-wood forests; also found along roadsides and streambanks.

GROWTH: An open, multi-stemmed small native tree or large shrub, up to 20 feet in height. Often leggy and unkempt-looking. The stems are tan to reddish-brown; tips develop a long, pointed bud in fall.

LEAVES: Smooth, light green leaves grow oppositely, attached to the stems by petioles (stemlets) that have flattened, wavy edges; leaves are narrowly elliptical, 2 to 5 inches long and one-half to one-third as wide. Bases are rounded to tapered; the tips taper to a sharp point. Leaves are glossy and hairless on both surfaces; edges are finely toothed. Leaves turn red in fall, and may be gone by the time the fruit ripens.

FRUIT: Oval to round drupes, about ½ inch long, grow in loose, flat clusters that hang from stem forks or tips; individual fruits may fall off before they are ripe, making the cluster look more open. Green fruits develop a reddish blush, then ripen to a dull blue-black. They eventually become black and wrinkled. Ripe nannyberries are delicious raw or cooked, but the pit is a nuisance. There are no toxic look-alikes; although fruits of some *Viburnums* such as downy arrowwood (pg. 238) taste awful, they aren't dangerous to sample—only unpleasant.

SEASON: Nannyberries ripen in late summer to early fall, and often persist through winter. Withered nannyberries, if still present on the plant in late fall or winter, make a tasty trail nibble.

COMPARE: Two plants in our area are similar. Blackhaw (*V. prunifolium*) appears in our area only in extreme southern Michigan and the south-eastern corner of Wisconsin. The petioles of blackhaw are broad and concave, and have smooth margins rather than the wavy margins of nannyberries; leaves are egg-shaped, 1 to 3 inches long and rounded at the tip. Withe-rod (pg. 204) has round petioles and oval to egg-shaped leaves; ripening fruits are hot pink. Fruits of both are edible and delicious.

NOTES: A delicious fruit, worth the trouble to remove the pit.

green = key identification feature

Wavy petiole,
pointed bud

TREE

ALTERNATE
LEAVES

MID TO
LATE SUMMER

Black Cherry –OR– **Rum Cherry**   *Prunus serotina*

HABITAT: Sun-dappled hardwood and mixed-wood forests; edge habitat.

GROWTH: A tall, stately native tree, up to 90 feet high and 50 feet wide but typically smaller; when young, may appear as a small shrub. Young stems are reddish-brown or gray, with prominent lenticels (breathing pores); older bark is dark gray, with curling, scaly plates.

LEAVES: Smooth, glossy leaves are oval, with tapered bases and a long, pointed tip; edges are finely toothed. Leaves are 2 to 5 inches long, one-half to one-third as wide, and dark green above, paler below. The base of the midrib on the underside has **fine reddish hairs** (visible with a lens); this is one of the easiest ways to positively identify a black cherry. Leaves grow alternately on a petiole (stemlet) that is up to 1 inch long.

FRUIT: Round, reddish-black drupes grow in **racemes** (long clusters of multiple fruits) from leaf axils. Fruits are about ⅓ inch in diameter; they are glossy but opaque. Fruit stemlets and the fruiting stalk are often reddish-purple. Black cherries are sweet and delicious, but the pit is fairly large in proportion to the flesh so the fruit is usually juiced, or pulped to make jam. There are no toxic look-alikes that are large trees, but there are several woody shrubs with inedible black fruits that could be confused with black cherries; please see below.

SEASON: Black cherries ripen in mid to late summer.

COMPARE: Chokecherries (pg. 136) have edible fruits that grow in racemes, but leaves are **wider** and **lack the hairs on the midrib.** Buckthorn (pgs. 130, 236 and 244) have mildly toxic red or black fruits; leaves are somewhat similar, but the fruits grow **singly or in clusters** from the leaf axils rather than in racemes.

NOTES: Black cherry leaves and pits contain hydrocyanic acid, a cyanide-producing compound. The leaves and pits should never be eaten, and care should be taken to avoid crushing cherry pits when juicing the fruits. Cooking or drying eliminates the harmful compound.

green = key identification feature

Hairs at base of midrib

TREE   ALTERNATE   LATE SUMMER
        LEAVES   TO EARLY FALL

Hackberry

Celtis occidentalis

HABITAT: Rich valleys and bottomlands; also hardwood forests, waste ground, fencerows and urban areas. Prefers moist soils, but can adapt to drier areas. Does best in full sun.

GROWTH: A small to medium-sized native tree, 40 to 60 feet in height with almost equal spread. Lower branches often droop toward the ground. Young stems are green to reddish-brown and knobby; branches are gray to brownish, with light-colored lenticels (breathing pores). Bark on the trunk is dark gray and ridged, with an unusual corky, warty texture.

LEAVES: Rough-textured, dull green leaves are shaped like an elongated heart, with a long, sharply pointed tip; undersides are pale. Leaves are 3 to 5 inches in length and about one-half as wide; they are widest near the base, which is rounded and often slightly angled. Edges have large, pointed teeth except around the base, which has smooth edges. Leaves grow alternately on medium-length petioles (stemlets); they often develop spots and galls in late summer.

FRUIT: Round drupes, ¼ to ⅓ inch in diameter, grow singly or in pairs on short stemlets from the leaf axils; they are purplish-black when ripe. The flesh is thin in comparison to the size of the pit; however, it is sweet and delicious. There are no toxic look-alikes that grow on trees.

SEASON: Fruits ripen in late summer to early fall, and may persist through winter if not eaten by birds and squirrels.

COMPARE: Black cherry (pg. 248) is a tree with small, round black fruits; however, its leaves are much narrower, and the fruits grow in long, hanging clusters. Sugarberry (*C. laevigata*) is a related species that is found primarily in the southeast; its northern range is central Missouri and southern Illinois. Ripe sugarberry fruits are dull orangish-brown.

NOTES: Hackberries are often planted in urban parks and along streets because they are fast-growing shade trees and resistant to storm damage. It is a good tree for the urban forager to learn; generally, only the birds and squirrels bother harvesting the fruit.

green = key identification feature

Hackberry bark

TENDER
LEAFY PLANT

ALTERNATE
LEAVES

SUMMER

Canada Mayflower
–OR– **False Lily of the Valley** *Maianthemum canadense*

HABITAT: This native species inhabits mixed, hardwood or coniferous forests; also occasionally found near bogs and swampy areas. It can grow in sun or shade.

GROWTH: An understory plant that is 3 to 7 inches in height. Thin stems grow from shallow underground rhizomes (root-bearing stems) that often form large colonies. Flowers and fruit are borne in clusters at the top of stems bearing two or three leaves. Stems with a single leaf do not flower.

LEAVES: One to three bright green, shiny leaves grow alternately from a single stem. Leaves are heart-shaped, with a deeply grooved midline and parallel veins that curve to meet at the sharply pointed tip. Bases are rounded and appear to clasp the stem. Most leaves appear to have a slight notch where the base joins the stem. Leaves are 1 to 3 inches long, and nearly as wide at the base. Edges are smooth.

FRUIT: Shiny, round berries are ⅛ to ¼ inch wide and cream-colored with red speckles most of the season. By late summer or early fall, berries soften and turn solid red. The ripe berries are bittersweet in flavor; they reportedly cause diarrhea, and consumption is not advised.

SEASON: In late spring or early summer, a cluster of white flowers grows at the top of stems bearing two or three leaves; the flowers turn into speckled cream-colored berries by midsummer. Berries turn pinkish with red speckles, then ripen to solid red by late summer or early fall.

COMPARE: Canada mayflower may be confused with three-leaved false Solomon's seal (*M. trifolium*), which is slightly less common; fruits are similar, but three-leaved false Solomon's seal has three narrow leaves, up to 6 inches long and one-quarter as wide. Bunchberry (pg. 86) has leaves that somewhat resemble those of Canada mayflower, but bunchberry plants have groupings of four to six leaves, with pronounced veins.

NOTES: Ruffed grouse and woodland rodents eat the berries.

green = key identification feature

Ripe fruit

TENDER
LEAFY PLANT

ALTERNATE
COMPOUND
LEAVES

MID TO
LATE SUMMER

White Baneberry
–OR– Doll's Eyes

Actaea pachypoda

HABITAT: This native plant grows in shady areas in moist hardwood and mixed forest. Often found in dappled woods alongside bracken fern and large-leaved aster.

GROWTH: Two to four doubly-compound leaves, each up to 15 inches long, grow alternately on the main stem; total height is 1 to 2½ feet. Flowers and fruits grow on a separate, leafless stalk that branches off one of the leaf stalks, and generally rise above the surrounding leaves.

LEAVES: Three large compound leaflets grow on each of the long leaf stalks that are attached alternately to the main stem; each has three or five smooth, sharply toothed leaflets oppositely attached by short stalks.

FRUIT: Firm, glossy white berry about ⅜ inch long, slightly oval to round with a shallow vertical groove. Each berry has a large, oval black dot at the bottom. The berries grow in a loose cluster at the top of the thin flower stalk, and are attached to the stalk by thick stemlets with slight knobs on both ends; stemlets are usually reddish-pink. Baneberries are toxic and should never be eaten.

SEASON: Berries ripen in mid to late summer.

COMPARE: The related red baneberry (pg. 74) looks similar, but the flower stalk and berry stemlets are thin and greenish, while those of white baneberry are much thicker and usually reddish-pink. Red baneberries generally have red berries, although they are sometimes white; regardless of color, the dot on the bottom of the red baneberry is much smaller than that on a white baneberry. Blue cohosh (pg. 186) has a similar form, but the leaves are rounded; fruits are larger and are blue when ripe.

NOTES: All parts of the plant are toxic. Ingestion of the berries leads to dizziness, vomiting or cardiac arrest; contact with leaves may cause skin irritation in sensitive individuals. Birds eat the berries with no ill effect, helping to disperse the seeds.

green = key identification feature

Pink berry stemlets

SMALL
WOODY SHRUB

ALTERNATE
COMPOUND
LEAVES

LATE SUMMER
THROUGH FALL

Western Poison Ivy

Toxicodendron rydbergii

HABITAT: This native plant (also listed as *Rhus radicans*) prefers partial sun and moist areas such as lake edges, streambanks and swamps. It can also be found in fields, ditches, parks and along trails.

GROWTH: Although it may look like a tender, leafy plant, western poison ivy is a perennial woody shrub that may grow to 4 feet high, although it is usually shorter. It has the classic three-part leaf configuration leading to the old saying, "Leaves of three, let it be."

LEAVES: Three-part leaves grow on the ends of long stalks attached alternately to the main stem. Petioles (stemlets) are often reddish where they join the leaflets, and the petiole of the middle leaflet is longer than those of the side leaflets. Leaflets are egg-shaped and 2 to 4 inches long, with irregular toothy or wavy edges; they sometimes have shallow lobes. Leaflets turn red in fall.

FRUIT: The round, ridged berries are greenish when immature, ripening to white or whitish-yellow. Berries grow in upright clusters near the main stem, and are about ³⁄₁₆ inch across; many plants have no berries, but must be avoided, regardless. All parts of the plant are toxic.

SEASON: Berries develop in late summer, and persist through fall.

COMPARE: Eastern poison ivy (pg. 42) is a vining plant with larger leaves and large, loose clusters of abundant greenish to yellowish-white berries that grow from leaf axils. Black raspberries (pg. 222), dewberries (pgs. 84, 232) and blackberries (pg. 234) often have toothy 3-part leaflets, but they are brambles with thorny stems; fruits are compound drupes.

NOTES: Both western and eastern poison ivy cause a painful rash. It usually takes multiple exposures to develop sensitivity, but a few people aren't allergic at all. The toxic compound, urushiol, remains active on everything it touches, until washed off. Wear gloves, long sleeves and pants when attempting to eliminate poison ivy. Pull or dig out the plants, transferring them to plastic bags for disposal; do not compost them. Never burn poison ivy, as the smoke may cause severe respiratory distress.

green = key identification feature

Ripe berries

VINING
SUBSHRUB

ALTERNATE
LEAVES

LATE SUMMER
THROUGH FALL

Creeping Snowberry

Gaultheria hispidula

HABITAT: Found in cool, damp woods, particularly in the northern boreal forest, creeping snowberry does well in acidic soils with dappled sunlight. Often associated with conifers and mosses on the edges of boggy or swampy areas. Frequently found growing on rotting logs.

GROWTH: Technically a subshrub, this native plant grows as a sprawling, ground-hugging vine, often in fairly dense mats. Stems have fine reddish hairs. Evergreen leaves remain on the plant all year. All parts of the plant typically have a mild wintergreen smell when bruised.

LEAVES: Alternate, oval to round, with a leathery texture, noticeably cleft midrib and slightly curled edges. Leaf tops are shiny, while undersides have scattered small, brownish, bristly hairs (visible with a lens). Leaves are typically about one-half the length of the berries.

FRUIT: Egg-shaped white fruit, ¼ to ⅜ inch long, on a very short stalk. The fruit has very fine hairs (visible with a lens). Fruits are edible, with a distinct wintergreen taste. There are no toxic look-alikes.

SEASON: Fruits appear in late summer and persist through fall.

COMPARE: Wild cranberry (three species; pg. 106) look similar when unripe, but leaves and stems are hairless and have no smell. Creeping wintergreen (pg. 110) is closely related, but its leaves are much larger; ripe berries are red. Common snowberry (pg. 262) has a similar name, but it is not related; it is a woody shrub up to 3 feet in height with much larger leaves, and its large, lumpy white berries are inedible.

NOTES: The berries make a refreshing trail nibble, and can be used to make unusual preserves. Leaves may be covered with boiling water and steeped for several hours to make a refreshing tea, which is sometimes used to relieve stomach upset. Like wintergreen, snowberry contains an aspirin-like compound, methyl salicylate, and should not be ingested by persons who are sensitive to aspirin. Creeping snowberry is a larval host for bog fritillary, a lovely orange and black butterfly found in the north.

green = key identification feature

LARGE
WOODY SHRUB

OPPOSITE
LEAVES

MID TO
LATE SUMMER

•see below

Dogwoods

Cornus spp.

HABITAT: Three species of white-fruited dogwood are common in our area. Gray dogwood (*Cornus racemosa*, pictured at right) is a native plant that grows in most of our area except for parts of northern Wisconsin and northern Michigan, including the Upper Peninsula. Native red-osier dogwood (*C. sericea*) and its non-native look-alike, Tatarian dogwood (*C. alba*), are found throughout our area. Dogwood prefers slightly damp soil, and is often found alongside swamps, road ditches and other wet areas.

GROWTH: A bushy shrub, typically 4 to 8 feet in height. Often grows in a spreading thicket. Stems of red-osier and some Tatarian dogwood turn intense red in fall and winter; mature stems of gray dogwood are gray.

LEAVES: Oppositely attached, 1 to 4 inches long and about one-half as wide, smooth edges, silvery-green undersides with fine hairs. Distinct veins curve in towards the pointy tip; gray dogwood leaves have three or four veins per side, while red-osier and Tatarian typically have five or six.

FRUIT: White, round drupes, ¼ inch across, with a small protrusion on the bottom; some fruits may be tinged with blue. The fruits grow in clusters on the ends of branching stemlets; gray dogwood clusters are rounded and pyramid-shaped, while those of red-osier and Tatarian dogwood are more flat-topped or slightly convex. The fruit stemlets of red-osier dogwood are greenish to purplish, while those of gray dogwood are bright red. Dogwood fruits are bitter and generally regarded as inedible.

SEASON: Fruits mature in mid to late summer.

COMPARE: Rough-leaved dogwood (*C. drummondii*) is found in only a few counties on the southern edges of Wisconsin and Michigan. Young stems are brownish-red and hairy; its leaves are coarsely textured, and the fruiting stems are bright red. Tatarian dogwood is often hybridized for the nursery trade, and these specimens have traits such as variegated leaves and more compact growth.

NOTES: Dogwood fruits are eaten by many birds, including cardinals, woodpeckers, wood ducks and upland birds; deer browse on the plants.

green = key identification feature

* combined range

Gray dogwood

LARGE WOODY SHRUB

OPPOSITE LEAVES

LATE SUMMER THROUGH FALL

Common   Western

Common Snowberry
–AND– **Western Snowberry**
Symphoricarpos spp.

HABITAT: Two native snowberry plants are found in our area: common snowberry (*Symphoricarpos albus*) and western snowberry (*S. occidentalis*, also called wolfberry). Both are found in open woods, ravines and prairies, as well as on hillsides and along edges of grasslands. They prefer well-drained soil, but will tolerate somewhat damp conditions.

GROWTH: Bushy, rounded shrubs; western snowberry is typically 2 to 5 feet in height, while common snowberry is 3½ feet or less. Both often form thickets. Twigs are slender and reddish-brown, with fine hairs; older branches are gray and have shreddy bark.

LEAVES: Oval to egg-shaped leaves grow oppositely on short, hairy petioles (stemlets); edges are often wavy. Leaves of western snowberry are up to 3 inches in length and roughly two-thirds as wide; common snowberry leaves are shorter, generally no more than 1½ inches long. Upper surfaces of both are blue-green to dark green, and may have scattered fine hairs; lower surfaces are generally hairy.

FRUIT: Roughly spherical, waxy white drupes, with a small floral remnant on the base, grow in tight clusters at the ends of branches or in leaf axils. Common snowberry fruits are often lumpy and misshapen, and up to ½ inch across; they are usually brilliant white. Western snowberry fruits are rounded, and up to ⅓ inch across; they are typically creamy white when young, turning purplish with age. Fruits of both are mildly bitter and are generally considered inedible; some sources list them as toxic.

SEASON: The fruits, which follow white to pinkish flowers, form in late summer, and may persist through winter on leafless branches.

COMPARE: Creeping snowberry (pg. 258) has a similar name, but it is not related; it is a trailing vine with tiny leaves, and edible oval white berries. All parts of creeping snowberry have a wintergreen smell when bruised.

NOTES: A winter food source for birds, including thrashers and upland birds.

green = key identification feature

Common snowberry

Western snowberry

TREE

ALTERNATE
COMPOUND
LEAVES

LATE SUMMER
THROUGH FALL

Poison Sumac

Toxicodendron vernix

HABITAT: Prefers shade and damp soil, and is often found at the edges of swamps or in poorly drained woods and bottomlands.

GROWTH: A small native tree up to 20 feet high, sometimes more like a large shrub, with red leaf stalks at the center of its compound leaves. Bark is grayish-brown and blotchy, with small raised bumps. Poison sumac often sends out branches from the base of the main trunk. Broken stems ooze a dark sap that is toxic.

LEAVES: Compound leaves grow alternately. Each leaf is 8 to 13 inches long, and has seven to 13 leaflets growing on short petioles. Leaflets are bright green, 2 to 4 inches long, smooth in texture with smooth, untoothed edges, and may be shiny on top. Poison sumac is very colorful in fall, with leaflets ranging in hue from yellow to orange to red to purple.

FRUIT: Round drupes are shiny and green when unripe, turning whitish-yellow by late summer; they are ¼ to ⅓ inch across. The fruits hang down in long, open clusters attached to leafless stems.

SEASON: Fruits ripen in late summer and may persist on the plant through winter, long after the leaves have fallen.

COMPARE: Smooth and staghorn sumac (pg. 164) have orange-to-red fruits; leaves have more leaflets, and leaflet edges are toothed.

NOTES: *All parts of poison sumac are toxic, and can cause severe allergic reactions.* The plant can be identified from a distance by the red leaf stalk, green to white fruits growing in a long, open cluster, and bright green or autumn-colored compound leaves. Stay away when you see these characteristics, as sensitive individuals may have a reaction merely by being close to the plant without even touching it. Burning the plants can cause respiratory distress in individuals a good distance away. Poison sumac is sometimes listed as *Rhus vernix*. No matter what it is called, this is a plant to avoid.

green = key identification feature

Fruit cluster

HELPFUL RESOURCES

Information on wild plants is readily available in books, magazines and on the internet. In general, information found on websites from University Extension Services, arboretums, colleges and other institutions of higher learning are generally more reliable than personal websites. Here is a list of some books and websites which provide good information, and which were helpful in writing this book.

WEBSITES

Andy's Northern Ontario Wildflowers, Andy Fyon, Sudbury, Ontario, Canada (ontariowildflower.com)

EDDMapS. 2017. Early Detection & Distribution Mapping System, The University of Georgia—Center for Invasive Species and Ecosystem Health. (eddmaps.org/distribution)

eFloras.org

Flora, Fauna, Earth and Sky … The Natural History of the Northwoods, Earl J.S. Rook (rook.org/earl/bwca/nature)

Illinois Wildflowers Info, Dr. John Hilty. (illinoiswildflowers.info)

Minnesota Wildflowers, Katy Chayka and Peter M. Dziuk. (minnesotawildflowers.info)

Missouri Plants, Dan Tenaglia. (missouriplants.com)

Montana Plant Life. (montana.plant-life.org)

Ontario Wildflowers and Trees, Walter Muma, Ontario, Canada. (ontariowildflowers.com, ontariotrees.com)

Robert W. Freckmann Herbarium, University of Wisconsin–Stevens Point, Stevens Point, WI 54481 (wisflora.herbarium.wisc.edu)

U.S. Department of Agriculture, NRCS. 2008. The PLANTS Database. National Plant Data Center, Baton Rouge, LA 70874. (plants.usda.gov)

U.S. Forest Service, Washington, D.C. 20250. (www.fs.fed.us/)

University of Connecticut Plant Database, Dr. Mark H. Brand. (hort.uconn.edu)

Virginia Tech, College of Natural Resources, Forestry Department, Blacksburg, VA 24061. (dendro.cnre.vt.edu/dendrology/main.htm)

BOOKS

Brill, Steven. *Identifying and Harvesting Edible and Medicinal Plants in Wild (and Not So Wild) Places*. New York: William Morrow, 1994.

Derig, Betty B. and Fuller, Margaret C. *Wild Berries of the West*. Missoula, MT: Mountain Press Publishing Company, 2001.

Elias, Thomas S. and Dykeman, Peter A. *Field Guide to North American Edible Wild Plants*. New York: Outdoor Life Books, 1982.

Lyle, Katie Letcher. *The Wild Berry Book: Romance, Recipes and Remedies*. Minnetonka, MN: NorthWord Press, 1994.

Marrone, Teresa. *Wild Berries & Fruits Field Guide: Illinois, Iowa and Missouri* (and *Indiana, Kentucky and Ohio*). Cambridge, MN: Adventure Publications, 2010 and 2011.

Peterson, Lee Allen. *A Field Guide to Edible Wild Plants of Eastern and Central North America*. Boston: Houghton Mifflin Company, 1977.

Petrides, George A. *A Field Guide to Trees and Shrubs*. Boston: Houghton Mifflin, 1958.

Rose, Francis. *The Wild Flower Key*. London, England: Frederick Warne, The Penguin Group, 1981.

Smith, Welby R. *Trees and Shrubs of Minnesota*. Minneapolis: University of Minnesota Press, 2000.

Symonds, George W.D. *The Shrub Identification Book* and *The Tree Identification Book*. New York: Harper Collins, 1963 and 1958.

Tekiela, Stan. *Wildflowers of Minnesota* (and *Michigan, Ohio* and *Wisconsin*). Cambridge, MN: Adventure Publications, 1999–2001.

Thayer, Samuel. *The Forager's Harvest* and *Nature's Garden*. Birchwood, WI: Forager's Harvest, 2006 and 2010.

GLOSSARY

Aggregate drupe: A fleshy fruit formed from a single flower, but composed of many drupes, each containing one seed; synonymous with compound drupe.

Alternate attachment: An arrangement of leaves in which individual leaves are attached to the stem in an alternating pattern, with some distance between each leaf. (*Compare:* Opposite attachment, Whorled attachment)

Annual: A plant which lives for one season only; reproduction is by seed rather than from roots. (*Compare:* Perennial)

Anther: The pollen-producing element of a flower.

Basal: Leaves growing at the base of a plant, often in a whorl or rosette pattern.

Berry: A simple, fleshy fruit containing one or more carpels, each with one or more seeds; the seeds are relatively soft. (*Compare:* Capsule, Cone, Drupe, Pepo, Pome, Pseudocarp)

Blade: The entire grouping of leaflets, stemlets and central leaf stalk that make up a compound leaf. The word "blade" is also used to describe the wide, flat part of a simple leaf.

Bloom: A light-colored or waxy coating on a fruit or stem that gives it a dusty appearance.

Boreal forest: A forest of the far north, characterized by coniferous trees, infertile soil and long, cold winters; the boreal forest is south of the Arctic Circle, in an area formerly covered by glaciers.

Bract: A petal-like structure at the base of a flower.

Bramble: A sprawling, vine-like shrub with arching branches that are generally thorny or prickly.

Cane: A flexible, woody stem; usually used to describe brambles such as raspberries.

Capsule: A dry, non-fleshy fruit that splits at maturity to scatter seeds. (*Compare:* Berry, Cone, Drupe, Pepo, Pome, Pseudocarp)

Carpel: Part of the ovary of a plant, containing ovules (eggs).

Cathartic: Purgative; causing diarrhea or vomiting.

Catkin: A spike-like structure with tiny unisexual flowers, often having a fuzzy appearance.

Clasping: A leaf that attaches directly to the stem, with no leaf stalk; the base of the leaf clasps, or slightly surrounds, the stem but does not extend beyond it. (*Compare:* Peltate, Perfoliate, Sessile)

Cleft: A linear depression with smooth edges.

Compound drupe: A fleshy fruit formed from a single flower, but composed of many drupes, each containing one seed.

Compound leaf: A leaf composed of a central leaf stalk with two or more leaflets. A compound leaf has a bud at its base; a leaflet does not. (*Compare:* Simple leaf)

Cone: A fruit consisting of scales arranged in an overlapping or spiral fashion around a central core; seeds develop between the scales. (*Compare:* Berry, Capsule, Drupe, Pepo, Pome, Pseudocarp)

Coniferous: A tree with needle-like or scale-like leaves (usually evergreen), whose seeds are contained in cones. (*Compare:* Hardwood)

Corymb: A flat-topped, umbrella-like cluster of multiple fruits, each growing on a stemlet that is attached to a single point on the central fruiting stalk; stemlets are varying in length so all fruits are on the same level. (*Compare:* Umbel)

Crown: A remnant of the flower, found on the base of some fruits; it looks like a circle of pointed, dried leaf tips. Also used to refer to the top of a tree or shrub, particularly one with a rounded appearance.

Dappled: A forested area that receives sunlight broken up by light leaf cover.

Deciduous: A tree or shrub whose leaves fall off at the end of the growing season. (*Compare:* Evergreen)

Dehiscent: A fruit that dries out and splits open to release its seeds; legumes are dehiscent. (*Compare:* Indehiscent)

Doubly-compound leaf: A compound leaf consisting of two or more compound blades, attached to the central leaf stalk. Only the main leaf stalk has a bud at the base; the secondary compound leaves are not true leaves, and have no bud.

Doubly-toothed leaf: Each leaf tooth has one or more smaller teeth, making for a very jagged edge that alternates between coarse and fine teeth.

Downy: Having fine, soft hairs.

Drupe: A simple, fleshy fruit with a hard pit (stone); the pit typically contains one seed, but can contain more. (*Compare:* Berry, Capsule, Compound drupe, Cone, Pepo, Pome, Pseudocarp)

Elliptic: A leaf that is roughly oval in shape; ends may be pointed or rounded.

Endangered: A native plant whose populations have been depleted by animal predation or over-harvesting, or whose growing area has been reduced by pollution, habitat loss or over-competition from other plants.

Evergreen: Leaves that remain green all year and do not fall from the plant; typically needle-like. (*Compare:* Deciduous)

Filament: A long stalk that holds the anther, the pollen-producing part of a plant.

Flower stalk: A separate stem that carries the flowers but no leaves. Synonymous with fruiting stalk.

Follicle: A dry fruit derived from a single carpel; follicles dry out and split open on one side only to release their seeds. (*Compare:* Legume, Nut)

Fruit: The ripened part of a plant that disperses seeds. (*See* Berry, Capsule, Cone, Drupe, Pepo, Pome, Pseudocarp)

Fruiting stalk: A separate stem that carries the fruits but no leaves. Synonymous with flower stalk.

Gall: A swelling in the stem of a plant, caused by an insect that has burrowed into the stem.

Gland: A cell, small organ or structure that secretes (discharges) minute amounts of fluids or other substances.

Hardwood: A broad-leaved tree whose seeds are contained in fruits or nuts. (*Compare:* Coniferous)

Indehiscent: A fruit that dries out but does not split open; nuts are indehiscent. (*Compare:* Dehiscent)

Introduced: A plant, often from Europe or Asia, that did not grow naturally in the wild in our area but was planted as an ornamental or a food crop; sometimes planted to control erosion or provide shade.

Invasive: A plant, generally non-native (introduced), that spreads rapidly and crowds out native plants, shades understory plants, changes soil chemistry or depletes soil of moisture.

Lance-shaped: A leaf that is long and slender, with sides that are almost parallel for much of the length.

Leaf axil: The point at which a leaf stalk (from a simple or compound leaf) joins the stem.

Leaflet: An individual leaf-like member of a compound leaf. A leaflet does not have a bud at its base; only true leaves such as the compound leaf and the simple leaf have a bud at the base.

Legume: A pod containing pea-like seeds; legumes dry out and split open to release their seeds. (*Compare:* Follicle, Nut)

Lenticel: A breathing pore, appearing as a bump or raised line in the bark of a tree or woody shrub.

Lobed leaf: A leaf that has several distinct sections, typically scalloped or pointed.

Midrib: The central rib of a leaf.

Mixed forest: A forest having both hardwood and coniferous trees.

Multiple fruit: A single fruit formed from multiple flowers that grow together in a cluster.

Node: A joining point, between a leaf stem and the main stem or between two stems.

Non-native: A plant, often from Europe or Asia, that did not grow naturally in the wild in our area but was planted as an ornamental or a food crop; sometimes planted to control erosion or provide shade.

Nut: A large, dry fruit with a hard seedcoat, usually containing a single seed; nuts are indehiscent. (*Compare:* Follicle, Legume)

Opposite attachment: An arrangement of leaves in which individual leaves are attached to the stem directly across from one another. (*Compare:* Alternate attachment, Whorled attachment)

Ovary: A case containing carpels, which hold the ovules (eggs); a component of the pistil.

Paddle-shaped: A leaf that is narrow at the base, widening at or above the midpoint to a broad tip that is typically rounded.

Palmately compound: An arrangement of leaflets in a compound leaf, in which individual leaflets radiate from a central point, similar to fingers radiating from the palm of a hand. (*Compare:* Pinnately compound)

Pectin: A natural thickening agent found in apples and some other fruits; pectin helps jelly and jam "set" or thicken naturally.

Peltate: A leaf whose stem is attached on the underside, slightly away from the base of the leaf. (*Compare:* Clasping, Perfoliate, Sessile)

Pepo: A simple fruit with a tough rind developed from the receptacle. (*Compare:* Berry, Capsule, Cone, Drupe, Pome, Pseudocarp)

Perennial: A plant whose greenery, flowers and fruit die back each season, but which grows again the following year from the same root. (*Compare:* Annual)

Perfoliate: A leaf whose base extends slightly beyond the stem, giving the impression that the stem is growing up through the leaf. (*Compare:* Clasping, Peltate, Sessile)

Petiole: The stemlet that attaches a leaf, or a leaflet, to the stem or leaf stalk.

Photosynthesis: The process by which a plant converts sunlight to food.

Pinnately compound: An arrangement of leaflets in a compound leaf, in which individual leaflets are arranged either alternately or oppositely along the central leaf stalk. (*Compare:* Palmately compound)

Pistil: The female part of a flower, consisting of an ovary, style and stigma; usually in the center of the flower.

Pome: A simple fruit whose flesh is developed from the receptacle. (*Compare:* Berry, Capsule, Cone, Drupe, Pepo, Pseudocarp)

Pseudocarp: A simple fruit, such as a pome or pepo, whose flesh is developed from a part other than the ovary. (*Compare:* Berry, Capsule, Cone, Drupe, Pepo, Pome)

Raceme: A long cluster of multiple fruits, each growing on a stemlet that is attached to a central fruiting stalk; stemlets are equal in length. (*Compare:* Umbrella-like cluster)

Receptacle: An enlarged area at the base of a flower, just below the reproductive structures. In compound drupes, the receptacle is the core of the fruit.

Rhizome: An underground stem that produces lateral shoots and roots at intervals.

Runner: A shoot growing from the base of a shrub, capable of rooting along its length.

Sepal: A type of petal in the outermost group at the base of a flower; typically green and leaf-like.

Serrated: Finely toothed.

Sessile: A leaf that attaches directly to the stem, with no leaf stalk. (*Compare:* Clasping, Peltate, Perfoliate)

Simple leaf: A single, true leaf with a bud at the base of the leaf stem. (*Compare:* Compound leaf, Leaflet)

Spadix: A club-like structure with many small flowers (later, fruits) clustered tightly together on a spike; usually partially enclosed by a spathe.

Spathe: A large petal-like structure, sometimes curled into a tube-like shape, that partially surrounds a flowering cluster called a spadix.

Stamen: The male part of a flower, consisting of the anther and filament; usually around the edges of the inside of a flower.

Stemlet: A secondary stem that connects a fruit or a leaf to the main stem.

Stigma: The part of a flower that collects and germinates pollen, which it then sends down the style into the ovules contained in the ovary.

Style: A long stalk that holds the stigma, which is the pollen-gathering part of a plant.

Subshrub: A perennial with a woody base and non-woody stems.

Sucker: A shoot that grows from the underground roots at the base of a plant; suckering plants often form thickets.

Tendril: A thread-like appendage, found on climbing vines, that coils around other plants or objects.

Terminal leaflet: The leaflet at the end of a compound leaf that has an uneven numbers of leaflets; other leaflets are paired.

Thicket: A dense cluster of shrubs, trees or brushy plants.

Toothed leaf: A leaf with multiple points (teeth) around the edge. Teeth can be sharply pointed or rounded. *See also* Doubly-toothed leaf.

Trifoliate: A compound leaf with three leaflets.

True leaf: A simple leaf, or a compound leaf, with a bud at the base. (*Compare:* Leaflet)

Tuber: A thickened portion of an underground stem, containing buds from which new growth will sprout; the common potato is a well-known tuber.

Umbel: A rounded, umbrella-like cluster of multiple fruits, each growing on a stemlet that is attached to a single point on the central fruiting stalk; stemlets are equal in length. (*Compare:* Corymb)

Umbrella-like cluster: A cluster of multiple fruits, each growing on a stemlet that is attached to a single point on the central fruiting stalk. If stemlets are equal in length, the cluster is rounded (umbel); if stalks are varying in length, the cluster has a flat top (corymb). (*Compare:* Raceme)

Whorled attachment: An arrangement of leaves in which three or more leaves attach to a central point. (*Compare:* Alternate attachment, Opposite attachment)

INDEX

275

ABOUT THE AUTHOR

Teresa Marrone has been gathering and preparing wild edibles for more than 20 years. She was formerly Managing Editor of a series of outdoors-themed books, and is the author of *Abundantly Wild: Collecting and Cooking Wild Edibles in the Upper Midwest*, as well as numerous other outdoors-related and regional cookbooks. Teresa has also written many magazine articles on wild foods and cooking, and has rekindled an early interest in photography.

Wild Berries & Fruits Field Guide of Minnesota, Wisconsin and Michigan combines her various skills and interests into a clear, concise, easy-to-use book that helps the user appreciate the diversity of the various wild berries and fruits that grow in this region. Teresa lives in Minneapolis with her husband, Bruce.

Further enhance your foraging and wild edibles knowledge with *Mushrooms of the Upper Midwest*. It's a visual guide to learning about nearly 400 species of common wild mushrooms.

Identify more than 150 species of common weeds: how each spreads, how to control it, and its possible benefits. The information is perfect for beginners and experts alike.